IMAGES OF WAR SPECIAL

M4 SHERMAN

Pat Ware

Illustrated by
Brian Delf

Pen & Sword
MILITARY

First published in Great Britain in 2014 by
PEN & SWORD MILITARY
an imprint of
Pen & Sword Books Ltd,
47 Church Street,
Barnsley,
South Yorkshire
S70 2AS

ISBN 978 1 78159 029 4

A CIP record for this book is available from the British Library.

Typeset by Chic Graphics

Printed and bound in India by Replika Press Pvt. Ltd.

Pen & Sword Books Ltd incorporates the Imprints of
Pen & Sword Aviation, Pen & Sword Family History, Pen & Sword Maritime, Pen & Sword Military, Pen & Sword Discovery, Wharncliffe Local History, Wharncliffe True Crime, Wharncliffe Transport, Pen & Sword Select, Pen & Sword Military Classics, Leo Cooper, The Praetorian Press, Remember When, Seaforth Publishing and Frontline Publishing.

For a complete list of Pen & Sword titles please contact
Pen & Sword Books Limited
47 Church Street, Barnsley, South Yorkshire, S70 2AS, England
E-mail: enquiries@pen-and-sword.co.uk
Website: www.pen-and-sword.co.uk

Contents

Chapter One

Development

With almost 50,0000 examples constructed over a four-year period between 1942 and 1945, the American M4 medium tank – these days universally known as the Sherman – was one of the most numerous and iconic tanks of the Second World War. The tank was manufactured at ten separate plants in the USA, as well as in Canada, and was used by the US and British Armies, and by all of the Western Allies. It was also supplied under US Lend-Lease arrangements to the Soviet Union and China, and was a decisive factor in turning the tide of war in north-west Europe.

However, although the Sherman was both reliable and easy to manufacture in large numbers, by the later years of the war it was under-gunned and under-protected when compared to the German *Tiger*, *Königstiger* and *Panther*. It also exhibited a distressing propensity for ammunition stored in the unprotected bins to catch fire. In truth, by 1944 the Sherman was outclassed in almost every respect, and the fact that the Allies prevailed says as much about the numbers of tanks available and the bravery of their crews as it does about the tanks themselves. Nevertheless, the simplicity and rugged reliability of the vehicle guaranteed a service life that spanned some forty or more years and, whilst it might not have been perfect, it did what it was designed to do, and it did it with the minimum of fuss. In addition, the chassis was also widely used as the basis for a number of self-propelled guns – 'gun motor carriages' in US Army parlance – as well as for a range of specialised armoured vehicles.

By the time development of the Sherman started in 1941, usable armoured fighting vehicles were scarcely twenty-five years old. British tanks had first been used in action on 15 September 1916, when thirty-six Mk I heavy tanks took part in what later came to be called the Battle of Flers-Courcelette. The action could scarcely have been considered successful, but it did at least persuade the military authorities that it was worth continuing the development of the tank – which, incidentally, had been so described in an attempt to conceal its true nature. By the second half of 1917 the Mk I had been superseded, in turn, by the Mks II, III and IV, the last named capable of being driven by one man, rather than the four that had formerly been required. The Mk V was introduced in July 1918 and was followed by the Mk V* and the Mk V**, both differing in detail only, with the Mk V** being the final iteration of the British heavy tank of the First World War.

During the final year of the conflict the American Expeditionary Force (AEF), which eventually consisted of a million men, fought alongside British and French troops in Europe. As a result of the need to move US troops into France as quickly as possible, the US Army's own heavy weapons were left behind, although the US Army had no domestic tank designs at the time. British Mk IV and Mk V tanks were shipped to the USA for training purposes, but the US Tank Corps was eventually equipped with a mix of British Mk V heavy tanks and French Renault FT-17 light tanks. In late 1918, with just months of war remaining, the British and US military authorities agreed that they would collaborate on the design and production of the Mk VIII Liberty tank. The theory was that the hulls and weapons would come from Britain, and would be united with American-made engines and transmissions in France; it was planned that around 4,500 examples would be constructed.

The Liberty project was cancelled when the war ended, but, nevertheless, the Americans constructed 100 of these tanks at the Rock Island Arsenal during 1919 and 1920, using them as the mainstay of the US Tank Corps until around 1932. Work had also started on a domestic version of the Renault FT-17 in 1917, with plans to construct a total of 4,000, but just sixty-four examples of what was known as the M1917 light tank had been constructed by the time the war ended. Eventually, a total of 1,100 of these tanks were built by Van Dorn Iron Works, the Maxwell Motor Car Company and the C.L. Best Tractor Company, and they continued to serve as the US Army's standard light tank into the 1930s.

In 1920 the National Defense Act, often referred to as the 'Kahn Act', reorganised the military and civilian arms of the US Army. One of the results of this reorganisation was that the development of tanks became the responsibility of the infantry divisions, and for this reason the tank was viewed as being primarily an infantry-support weapon, with the General Staff defining the role of the tank as being 'to facilitate the uninterrupted advance of the rifleman in the attack'. Future tanks were described as being either 'light', which meant weighing less than 5 tons, or 'medium', the latter being restricted to a maximum of 15 tons in order not to overload existing military bridging equipment.

A year earlier, in 1919, the US Ordnance Department had started work on the design of a new medium tank that was similar in arrangement to the British Medium D, which many consider to be the ultimate British tank design of the First World War. Two pilot models were authorised for construction on 13 April 1920, the first of which was described as the 'medium A tank M1921'; the second, known as the 'medium tank M1922', used an alternative form of track and suspension. However, problems with the Murray & Tregurtha engine, which was simply a modified marine unit, eventually led to the Packard Motor Company being awarded a contract to develop a purpose-designed tank engine. The pace of development was not exactly rapid and it was not until 1927 that the 'medium A tank M1921', with the Packard engine installed and with other detail changes, became the T1.

Following a period of appraisal, the Ordnance Committee recommended that the T1 be standardised – meaning that it was officially adopted by the US Secretary of War as the preferred, or 'standard', vehicle for the stated role – as the 'medium tank M1'. The classification was withdrawn a few months later, but the sole example of the tank continued to be used as a test bed; in 1932 the Packard engine was replaced by a Liberty L-12 unit, and at the same time the designation was changed to T1E1. Originally designed for use in aircraft, the V12 Liberty engine produced around 338bhp from a capacity of 27 litres, but unfortunately the additional power led to numerous drive-line failures.

At the same time Rock Island Arsenal had also been working on the development of a new 15-ton medium tank, designated the T2. When the T2 prototype finally appeared in 1929/30, it bore more than a passing resemblance to the British Vickers medium tank of 1922/23. The riveted hull was constructed from a maximum 22mm of armour, and the tank was armed with a 47mm gun in a small rotating turret, together with a co-axially mounted 0.50in machine gun; there was also a 37mm gun, together with a 0.30in machine gun, mounted in a sponson on the right-hand side. The prototype was extensively tested during 1931, but was never recommended for standardisation.

Between 1921 and 1936 the US Ordnance Committee spent a considerable amount of time testing and evaluating the so-called 'convertible' tanks constructed by Walter J. Christie's Front Drive Motor Company. These were designed to be able to operate with equal facility on or off their tracks; it was hoped that by running tanks on wheels whenever possible, it would help to avoid the inevitable breakdowns and mechanical failures associated with early track-laying vehicles, as well as obviating the need for specialised tank transporters. The first of these, the M1919, was demonstrated at Aberdeen Proving Ground in January 1921, driving a total of 374 miles, of which just 10 per cent involved the use of the tracks. Modifications were made later that year and the rebuilt vehicle, now designated M1921, was subjected to a further round of testing before being rejected as unsuitable. The same fate awaited the further-modified M1922.

No doubt smarting from the rejection of his M1921/22 models, Christie set about reorganising his Front Drive Motor Company as the US Wheel Track Layer Corporation, at the same time moving from Hoboken, New Jersey, to Rahway. On 28 October 1928 Christie demonstrated a new tank, the M1928, at Fort Myer,

Virginia. The convertible wheel/track facility was retained, but the M1928 also incorporated a new high-speed suspension system that employed four large-diameter independently sprung rubber-tyred wheels on each side. Each wheel was mounted on a trailing arm suspended on a large coil spring. During its period of testing the tank was driven from Fort Meade to Gettysburg, a distance of almost 70 miles, making the outward trip on its wheels, achieving a maximum speed of almost 70mph at times, and returning on tracks, when the maximum speed was a more modest 42mph. Impressed, the Ordnance Department issued a contract for a single vehicle, now designated M1931, followed by a further seven, by which time it had become the 'convertible medium tank T3'. Further developments and modifications saw the designation change to T3E1, T3E2 and finally T3E3.

During 1935/36 a further sixteen Christie tanks were constructed at Rock Island Arsenal. Powered by a Continental radial petrol engine producing 268bhp, and designated 'medium tank T4', these vehicles for the first time incorporated a controlled-differential steering system in place of the crude brake-and-clutch design that had been used on earlier tanks. Three examples were also produced of a modified version, designated T4E1, that incorporated a barbette structure on the upper hull in place of the turret. Although both designs were recommended for standardisation, the vehicles were not accepted for service on the grounds of their excessive cost, and the fact that they were felt to be underpowered.

Having rejected Christie's designs as unsuitable, in May 1936 the Ordnance Committee took a new approach, and recommended the development of a new design, designated the 'medium tank T5'. Essentially a larger version of the successful M2 light tank, of which it used many of the same components, including the vertical volute spring suspension (VVSS) system, the T5 should be considered as the first step along the road that eventually led to the design of the Sherman M4 medium tank.

During trials the T5 was considered to be underpowered but, following the replacement of the 250bhp Continental air-cooled radial engine with a Wright radial that was able to produce better than 350bhp, the design was standardised as the 'medium tank M2'. The turret was supported on a full-width barbette, and the main gun was the 37mm M6 weapon; production versions also carried eight 0.30in machine guns placed so as to provide 360-degree coverage. A total of fifteen tanks were produced at Rock Island Arsenal before the design was modified by increasing the width of the tracks, improving the armoured protection and increasing the power output of the engine to 400bhp. In this form the vehicle was designated M2A1 and in 1940 a contract was awarded to the Chrysler Corporation to build 1,000 tanks at a rate of 100 a month ... at the yet-to-be-erected Detroit Tank Arsenal.

By this time the weight limit for 'medium' tanks had been increased and American tank doctrine now viewed the 'medium' tank in the same way that the British used their 'cruisers' ... US Field Manual FM100-5 described the role of the armoured division as being 'organized primarily to perform missions that require great mobility and firepower ... it is given decisive missions ... it is capable of engaging in all forms of combat, but its primary role is in offensive operations against hostile rear areas'. Clearly, the medium tank was now seen as a 'striking' vehicle rather than being reserved for infantry support.

However, even before the M2A1 went into production, German *Blitzkrieg* tactics in France and the Low Countries during 1940 showed beyond any shadow of doubt that the 37mm gun was inadequate, and in August 1940 the decision was taken to upgrade the medium tank to carry a 75mm gun. Chrysler's contract was cancelled. It was equally clear that the larger gun could not be fitted into the turret of the M2A1 and work started immediately on designing a new tank to be known as the M3 medium. Based on the agreed mechanical specification of the M2A1 but with a 75mm gun mounted in a sponson, and with a 37mm gun in a rotating turret, the M3 was identified by the British, who started taking deliveries of these tanks in mid-1941, as the General Lee and the General Grant, depending on the exact configuration of the turret. The curious arrangement of guns and turrets made for a very high profile and this, combined with the limited traverse of the main gun, meant that, at best, the M3 could not be considered as anything other than a stopgap measure. Nevertheless, the vehicle remained in production until December 1942, and a total of 6,258 examples were produced.

Once the design work for the M3 was under way, the Armored Force Board set about drawing up a specification for its successor, at first designated the 'T6 medium tank'. Design proposals had been prepared by Rock Island Arsenal by April 1941 and, although it was initially based on the lower hull and automotive equipment of the M3, the M4 was an altogether better machine, with a cast or welded upper hull mounting a fully rotating powered turret. Heavy hinged access doors were provided on either side of the hull as with the M3, and the number of crew members was reduced to five. The main gun was to be the long-barrelled M3 75mm weapon that was still in development, carried in what was described as the T48 mount, together with a 0.30in co-axial machine gun. There was also a rotating cupola on the right-hand side of the turret roof mounting a 0.30in anti-aircraft machine gun, and three more machine guns in the bow, two in a tandem mount. Other possible weapon arrangements that were considered included two 37mm guns, together with a single 0.30in machine gun; a 105mm howitzer and an 0.30in machine gun; three 0.50in machine guns in an anti-aircraft mount; and a British 6-pounder (57mm) gun with a co-axial 0.30in machine gun.

The M2A1 was replaced by the M3, which was identified by the British as the General Lee or General Grant, according to the turret configuration. The M3 followed the agreed mechanical specification of the M2A1, but was armed with a 75mm gun in a side sponson, and a 37mm gun in a rotating turret. The photograph shows a US Army M3 General Lee, lacking its 37mm gun. (*US Signal Corps*)

A simple wooden mock-up was built during the following month and was shown to the Armored Force Board for approval. Following this inspection, some detail changes were requested, and an engineering model was produced at Aberdeen Proving Ground during September with a cast hull. The long-barrelled 75mm M3 gun was not yet ready for production, and this engineering model (and the first two Shermans to be produced) was fitted with the shorter-barrelled M2, which necessitated the addition of twin counterweights at the muzzle end of the barrel to balance the weapon in its mount. The turret, which was also of cast construction, allowed space for radio sets to be installed in the bustle and in the right-hand sponson, with the brackets allowing both American and British sets to be used.

At the same time Rock Island Arsenal was asked to build a second engineering model, this time with a welded hull assembled from separate pieces of face-hardened steel armour, although no turret was required. The Aberdeen-produced pilot was shown to personnel of the Armored Force Board, and some further minor modifications were requested, including the elimination of the vulnerable side access doors and the removal of the turret-mounted cupola, the latter involving some reshaping of the turret roof. The T6 was standardised as the 'M4 medium tank' in September 1941, with the recommendation that a 0.50in anti-aircraft machine gun be mounted on the turret roof, and that a ball mount be provided for the right-hand bow machine gun. By the following month these changes had been made, and the first production pilot models were commissioned during November and December 1941. It was planned that during 1942 the M4 – dubbed General Sherman or, more usually, simply Sherman by the British, a name that was not widely used by the Americans until the post-war years – would eventually be introduced to all of the production facilities that were currently building the M3.

When production started, it was with the cast-hull variant, designated M4A1. The welded-hull version was described as the M4, and subsequent variants were designated M4A2, M4A3, M4A4 and M4A6; the M4A5, which also had a cast hull, was constructed in small numbers in Canada and was named Grizzly. The British Army described the M4 as the Sherman I, and the M4A1 as the Sherman II; as new variants were produced, the designations became Sherman III, IV, V and VII; the designation Sherman VI was allocated to the Canadian-built Grizzly, but the designation was not used by the British Army.

Manufacturing of the M4A1 started at the Lima Locomotive Works, Ohio, in February 1942 on an assembly line that had been established to fulfil a British contract. The first tank off the line was retained by the US Ordnance Board for test purposes, while the second (numbered T25190 by the British War Office) was shipped to London, where it was given the name 'Michael' in honour of the work of

Cast-hull M4A1s photographed during a disembarkation exercise; note the one-piece cast nose that replaced the earlier three-piece assembly. The lead tank lacks the ball-mounted bow machine gun. (*US Navy*)

Michael Dewar, head of the British Tank mission in the USA, and was displayed on Horseguards Parade. A month later production was also started at the Pressed Steel Car Company of New Jersey. By October the Sherman had seen its first combat, when three British regiments fielded 150 Shermans alongside British Crusaders at the battle of El Alamein. With its ability to fire both high-explosive and armour-piercing ammunition, the Sherman was able to effectively cover both the infantry support and tank-on-tank combat roles, although US tank doctrine still doggedly maintained that tank-on-tank combat was a rare occurrence.

Like the M3 before them, the M4 and M4A1 Shermans were powered by a rear-mounted Wright, later Continental, R-975-EC2 nine-cylinder air-cooled radial engine producing a maximum of 400bhp at 2,400rpm. The early EC2 variant of the engine was subsequently replaced by the R-975-C1, which produced the same power but had a lower compression ratio, making it suitable for use with lower octane fuels. The C1 was eventually superseded by the C4, in which the power output was increased to 460bhp. The engine was coupled to the front sprockets through a twin-plate dry clutch and a five-speed manual transmission with a single reverse gear. The track runs were supported on three bogie units, each consisting of a pair of in-line rubber-tyred wheels carried on swinging arms and suspended on vertical volute springs. Each bogie unit also carried a track-return roller on its upper face. By the summer of 1942 a new design of track-return roller was being used, with the roller mounted on the rear face of each suspension unit; a spring pad was fitted to the top of the suspension unit in place of the roller. Steering was by controlled differential.

After just two tanks had been constructed, the short-barrelled M2 gun was superseded by the M3, and at the same time a rotor shield was added to the gun mount to reduce the possibility of small arms fire preventing movement of the main gun, and to prevent bullet splash from entering the fighting compartment. The T48 mount was now standardised as the M34. In 1943 the 75mm M3 gun was superseded by the 76mm M1, mounted in an improved turret with an integral counterweight; this was described as the Sherman IIA by the British. There was also a howitzer variant, equipped with a 105mm M4 gun, which was described as the Sherman IIB.

Secondary armaments included four 0.30in Browning machine guns: one fitted co-axially to the left of the main gun; two in a tandem mount in the centre of the lower hull, which could be locked in position anywhere between +8 degrees and −6 degrees elevation; and a fourth gun in the right-hand side of the hull intended to be operated by the co-driver. The twin bow machine guns were omitted from March 1942 onwards. One 0.50in heavy machine gun was carried in an anti-aircraft ring mount surrounding the split hatch that had replaced the rotating cupola in the turret roof; this gun was superseded by a 0.30in weapon between September 1942 and February 1943, at which time the 0.50in gun was reinstated.

The hull was revised when the original three-piece cast differential housing was replaced by a one-piece casting that made it easier to assemble the transmission, as well as providing additional stiffness. The shape of the casting was subsequently amended to give a sharper, stronger profile.

In May 1942 the Washington-based Pacific Car & Foundry Company also started building the M4A1, continuing until November 1943. Although their hull casting retained the apertures for the twin bow machine guns, these weapons had already been eliminated. The Pressed Steel Company, which had been building the welded-hull M4 since March 1942, started to also produce the cast-hull M4A1 in July 1942; by the time production of the M4A1 ended in December 1943, the three companies had built 6,281 examples between them.

The M4 (Sherman I) was similar in most respects to the M4A1, aside from the welded hull, which provided a little more space for the crew and additional space for ammunition stowage. As with the M4A1, the three-piece differential housing was superseded by a one-piece casting, while late production M4s constructed at the Detroit Tank Arsenal used a hybrid cast/welded form of construction in which the upper front part of the hull was formed from a single casting that was welded to the remainder of the hull ahead of the turret ring. These were designated the Sherman Hybrid I by the British.

Alongside production at Pressed Steel, the M4 was also built by the Baldwin Locomotive Works, the American Locomotive Company, Pullman-Standard and the Chrysler Detroit Tank Arsenal. The total number of M4s constructed with the M3 75mm gun was 6,748, and the Detroit Tank Arsenal constructed a further 1,641 examples with the 105mm M4 howitzer (Sherman IB). No M4s were fitted with the 76mm gun.

By late 1941 it had become obvious that existing production facilities were not able to manufacture the Sherman in sufficient numbers and plans were put in hand for a modified version of the welded-hull M4 tank to be produced by General Motors using the company's 6046D liquid-cooled diesel engine set-up that had been developed for the earlier M3A3/M3A5 tank. The size of the power plant, which consisted of a pair of GM 6-71 two-stroke diesel truck engines installed side-by-side, necessitated modifications to the engine compartment. Each engine had its own clutch, with the power transmitted through a helical drive train to a collector gear and thence to the transmission; in extremis it was possible to drive the tank using just one of the engines. The resulting vehicle was designated M4A2 (Sherman III to the British, or Sherman IIIA when fitted with the 76mm gun).

A pilot vehicle was ready by the spring of 1942 and was shipped to Aberdeen Proving Ground, where, despite initial criticism, subsequent trials demonstrated that it was more powerful than either the M4 or M4A1 and offered similar levels of reliability, although the engine was considered to be susceptible to excessive levels of dirt in the air intakes. Production also started almost immediately at the Pullman-Standard Car Company and at the GM Fisher Tank Arsenal at Grand Blanc, Michigan. Later that year three additional plants were also brought on-stream to manufacture the M4A2, with production starting at the American Locomotive Company in September, at the Baldwin Locomotive Works in October and at Federal Machine & Welder in December. The M4A2 was actually the first of the welded-hull Sherman variants to go into production, beating the M4 by two or three months, and total production amounted to 10,968 units between April 1942 and May 1944. Of these, 8,053 were equipped with the original 75mm M3 gun, the remainder (2,915) having the 76mm M1 gun in the improved turret.

The adoption of the GM 6046D power plant had brought about a useful increase in the number of tanks being produced, but it was still not sufficient to satisfy the demand, and in the spring of 1942 the Ford Motor Company produced three pilot models of what became known as the M4A3 (Sherman IV; Sherman IVA with the 76mm gun; Sherman IVB with the 105mm howitzer). The hull was the welded design that had been used for the M4 and the M4A2, with a one-piece cast differential housing, and the tank rode on a modified, heavy-duty version of the VVSS suspension with larger diameter springs. Power came from a 500bhp Ford GAA-III V8 petrol engine, effectively a modified version of a V12 engine that Ford had originally developed for use in aircraft. The GAA-III engine had already been trialled in the M3E1 tank before being authorised for use in the Sherman in January 1942.

The three pilot models, each using a slightly different variation of the engine, were shipped to the General Motors Proving Ground for trials in late May 1942. Early results suggested that the engine was not sufficiently reliable, there were structural weaknesses in the crankcase, as well as in the crankshaft itself, and the engine had a propensity for burning exhaust valves as well as an appetite for head gaskets. It wasn't until June 1943 that Aberdeen Proving Ground was able to report that not only was the engine considered to be 'very satisfactory' for medium tanks, but that it was also more easily maintained and serviced than the other engines currently in use. Production started almost immediately and the M4A3 became the *de facto* standard Sherman variant for the US Army. In common with the M4A1 and the M4A2, the original 75mm M3 gun was superseded by the 76mm M1 in the new turret in September 1943; at the same time, after building 1,690 examples of the M4A3 with the 75mm gun, production at Ford was completely halted, although the company did continue to build the GAA-III engine for use by the other manufacturers constructing the M4A3. As well as Ford's output, the Chrysler Detroit Tank Arsenal built 4,017 examples equipped with the 76mm gun, and 3,039 with the 105mm howitzer, while the GM Fisher Tank Arsenal built 3,071 with the 75mm gun, and 525 with the 76mm gun.

By the summer of 1943 the Ford engine was considered the standard power plant for the Sherman, performing better in trials than the Wright/Continental radial, which was its only serious rival. Continuous modification had eliminated most of the design weaknesses and the engine was able to both meet and exceed the 400-hour endurance requirement. Total production of the M4A3 came to 12,342 examples, and it is claimed that had sufficient production capacity been available, all Shermans produced after the autumn of 1943 would have been equipped with the Ford engine.

During the spring of 1944 the Fisher Tank Arsenal constructed 254 examples of the unique M4A3E2 assault tank – often described, unofficially, as the 'Jumbo' or 'Cobra King'. The variant was intended for an infantry support role during the invasion of Europe, when the US Army believed that they would come up against large numbers of German heavy tanks. Features included a hull that had been up-armoured on all surfaces, and a new heavy turret mounting the 75mm M3 gun; some units replaced this in the field with the slightly better 76mm gun. The considerable increase in weight reduced the top speed to 22mph.

However, the numbers being produced were still not enough, but a shortage of engine production capacity meant that it was not possible to simply build the tanks at more locations. So serious were the problems relating to production that in June 1942, having learned that 3,500 GM diesel engines had been diverted to the Navy, General John K. Christmas, Chief of the Ordnance Board, was reported as having said:

> We cannot stand any more diversions of engines and still meet the 1942 tank objectives ... they are continually calling me into meetings where they want to take the Wright [or Continental] engine and put it into training planes ... fifty per cent of the tanks made this year will have Wright engines, thirty-four per cent will have General Motors engines, ten per cent will have Chrysler, and six per cent will have Ford. So, if they start taking away General Motors and Wright engines, they are taking away the foundation of the program.

The Chrysler engine to which Christmas referred was the A-57 multi-bank engine that had originally been developed for use in the M3A4 and which, it was felt, might also be suitable for the Sherman. In fact, the use of this power unit had been approved back in February 1942, resulting in the M4A4 (Sherman V) variant.

The M4A4 also used the welded hull of the M4, although in this case the frontal section consisted of five major sections rather than seven and the overall length of the hull was extended at the rear to accommodate the huge engine assembly. This also meant that the suspension bogie units were spaced further apart. The A-57 engine consisted essentially of five six-cylinder motor car engines, each of 4,107cc capacity, assembled onto a common crankcase in a star configuration; each of the five cylinder banks had its own carburettor and distributor, and the crankshafts were geared together to allow the whole contraption to operate as a single unit. Early examples even used five separate belt-driven water pumps, but in the production version there was a single pump, driven by a gear train. The combined power output from the thirty cylinders was 425bhp and, although physically large and heavy, the device was actually tolerably reliable. The US Desert Warfare Board had dubbed the M4A4 'unsatisfactory for combat', but it was favoured by the British, and the Royal Electrical & Mechanical Engineers (REME) reported that the engine was 'very reliable' and, providing sodium-filled exhaust valves were used, had a life in excess of

2,000 miles – this compares to less than 1,000 miles for the nine-cylinder radial, which was also said to be rather prone to breaking down if used to slow the vehicle when descending hills. Oil consumption was similarly reduced and, surprisingly, considering the complexity of the design, the demand for maintenance was not excessive.

A pilot model had been produced by May 1942 and the first production model was completed alongside the M3A4 on 22 July. By 3 August production of the old M3A4 had been terminated and the switch to full production of the M4A4 was made without 'losing a tank'. The M4A4 remained in production until September 1943, and by the time production ended a total of 7,499 examples had been constructed.

The designation of the next variant, the M4A5, tends not to appear in much period documentation covering the M4 family, presumably because it was built only in Canada and in comparatively small numbers. It is frequently (and erroneously) referred to as the Ram II, which was actually a Canadian-built version of the American M3 medium tank. Admittedly, the Ram did employ a somewhat Sherman-shaped cast hull, albeit with a larger turret mounting a British 6-pounder (57mm) gun.

The M4A5 had evolved out of a scheme to standardise the armoured fighting vehicles being produced in the USA, Britain and Canada, and was originally to have been named Buffalo. This name was subsequently dropped in deference to the British 79th Armoured Division, which used a buffalo as its divisional sign, and the vehicle became known as the 'Grizzly cruiser tank'.

In March 1942, during preliminary discussions, it was agreed that the M4A5 would be based largely on the cast-hull Sherman M4A1, albeit with a thicker hull (75mm rather than 51mm) and, like the M4A1, it would be powered by the Wright or Continental R-975 radial engine. It was also to be armed with the M3 75mm gun mounted in the same turret as that used for the M4A1. However, it differed from the standard M4A1 Sherman by having seventeen teeth on the drive sprocket rather than the standard thirteen, in order to match the shorter-pitch Canadian dry-pin (CDP) track, which, incidentally, required no rubber. It also featured what were described as 'British stowage arrangements', consisting of a large box on the rear of the turret. The original production plan called for 1,200 Grizzlies to be built at the Montreal Locomotive Works, where it replaced the Canadian Ram II on the production line. By the middle of January 1943 around 80 per cent of the parts required were said to have been ordered, with the view that the tanks would be completed by February 1944. However, just 188 examples had been produced between August and December 1943, with the first batch of twenty-three delivered during the third week of October, when it was decided that the Montreal

Known as 'Grizzly', the M4A5 used the same type of cast hull as the M4A1, and was constructed by the Montreal Locomotive Works. Just 188 examples were built, all of which were armed with the 75mm gun. (*Warehouse Collection*)

Locomotive Works would cease production of the Grizzly and concentrate instead on producing 25-pounder field guns and the Sexton self-propelled gun Mk II which used the chassis of the Ram II. The Grizzly hull was also used as the basis for the Skink 20mm quad anti-aircraft tank, of which just three examples were built. Some Grizzlies were shipped to Britain, while others remained in Canada, where they were used for training.

The last variant of the M4 gun tank was the M4A6 (there was no British Sherman VI – the allocation would have been applied to the M4A5 – and the M4A6 was designated the Sherman VII). Starting life as the experimental M4E1, the M4A6 was effectively an M4A4 hybrid (cast/welded) hull into which had been fitted a diesel multi-fuel version of the Wright G-200 air-cooled supercharged radial engine. The necessary conversion work on the engine was carried out by the Caterpillar Tractor Company, and the resulting power unit was identified as the D-200A, later designated the 'Ordnance engine RD-1820'. Maximum power output was 450bhp and the engine was equally capable of running on crude oil, diesel fuel, aviation spirit, or petrol of up to 100-octane rating. Caterpillar installed twenty of these engines into standard M4A4 hulls that had been constructed at the Detroit Tank Arsenal specifically for the purpose during late 1942 and, following a period of trials, a contract was issued for 1,000 engines to be built. Arrangements were made to install 775 engines into late version M4A4 hulls, with a one-piece cast front, and with *appliqué* armour on the hull sides; a rounded blister was required on the engine deck to accommodate the height of the radial engine.

Ten examples were submitted to the Armored Force Board during the spring of 1944 for a further period of testing, and were shown to run satisfactorily on 72- or 80-octane fuel mixed with 10 per cent of lubricating oil. Despite some problems with wear of the cylinder walls, the tank went into production with the RD-1820 engine as the M4A6 at the Detroit Tank Arsenal in late 1943, but in February 1944 the contract was cancelled after just seventy-five examples had been constructed.

Tests carried out at Fort Knox during the spring of 1944 concluded that the M4A6 offered the best levels of performance and fuel economy of any of the Sherman variants but, despite this brief flirtation with multi-fuel engines, the M4A6 was reclassified as 'limited standard' in May 1945. The US Army reverted to petrol-engined tanks, and continued to favour petrol as the primary battlefield fuel for the next ten or fifteen years. And, despite the M4A6 being given the British designation 'Sherman VII', none was operated by the British Army ... indeed, none came to Britain at all since all were assigned to training units in the USA before being subsequently used as hard targets or scrapped!

During the First World War the American Expeditionary Force (AEF) in Europe was equipped with British Mk V heavy tanks. In mid-1918 the British and US military authorities agreed to collaborate on the design and production of the Mk VIII Liberty tank (*seen here*). Some 4,500 examples were planned, with the hulls and weapons coming from Britain, and the engines and transmissions from the USA. The project was cancelled when the war ended, but 100 of these tanks were constructed at the Rock Island Arsenal during 1919/20. (*Warehouse Collection*)

Alongside the British heavy tanks, the US Army also deployed the Renault FT-17 light tanks. There were plans to build 4,000 examples in the USA under the designation M1917, but in the end just sixty-four were constructed. (*Warehouse Collection*)

A contract for 1,000 examples of the US Army's M2 medium tank, in its uprated M2A1 form, was awarded to the Chrysler Corporation in 1940. By August it had become clear that the M2A1 was effectively obsolete in the face of German tank advances and the contract was cancelled, with work beginning immediately on its replacement. Just ninety-four M2A1s were built. (*Warehouse Collection*)

The M3 was never considered as more than an interim model and work began immediately on its replacement – initially known as the T6, but later designated M4 or General Sherman. This wooden mock-up was constructed in May 1941 for approval by the US Armored Force Board. The lower hull of the M3 was carried over, but the sponson-mounted gun was omitted, and the 75mm main gun fitted into a fully rotating powered turret. (*Warehouse Collection*)

Development of the long-barrelled M3 75mm gun planned for the Sherman was not completed in time, and the first two tanks to be constructed were armed with the short-barrelled M2 version. Large counterweights had to be fitted to the end of the barrel to balance the weapon in its mount. (*Warehouse Collection*)

On paper, the first variant of the Sherman was the welded-hull M4, although in fact this was not the first type into production. In this photograph of an early M4, the short-barrelled M2 75mm gun has been replaced by the long-barrelled M3, and the twin bow machine guns, which were fitted until March 1942, have been omitted. (*US Signal Corps*)

The cast-hull M4A1 was actually the first Sherman variant into production, with supplies destined for the British Army. The photograph shows the first example to be constructed at the Lima Locomotive Works in Ohio. (*Warehouse Collection*)

A mid-production M4A1, showing the 76mm gun; the engine decks are not original. Like many retired Shermans, this tank serves as a static monument to the sacrifices of so many during the years 1939 to 1945. (*Ian Young*)

The M4A2 reverted to the welded hull. This example, which has the sharper one-piece nose casting, was one of 540 constructed by Federal Machine & Welder. (*US Signal Corps*)

An M4A2 with the 76mm gun; note the wider tracks that are indicative of the improved HVSS suspension. This example also has the travelling lock, in the form of a large clamp that secures the gun barrel while travelling. (*Warehouse Collection*)

The M4A3 was the fifth Sherman variant to enter production and, with its powerful V8 petrol engine, was the type most favoured by the US Army. This example was constructed by the Ford Motor Company and the number '5' on the side of the hull would suggest that it was the fifth off the line. (*Ford Motor Company*)

Rear view of the M4A3 105mm, showing the wide tracks and HVSS suspension system. The louvred exhaust deflectors at the rear are not standard equipment. (*Warehouse Collection*)

The M4A3E8 was the 1944 prototype for the 76mm gun variant of the M4A3, with HVSS suspension and wet ammunition stowage facilities. Known by the US Army as the 'Easy Eight', this was the variant favoured by the US into the post-war years. (*US Signal Corps*)

(*Opposite top*) An early Chrysler-powered M4A4 with the M2A1 105mm short-barrelled howitzer that was subsequently redesigned due to access problems that made loading difficult inside the tank. (*US Signal Corps*)

(*Opposite below*) Standardised in 1943, the standard 105mm howitzer for the Sherman was the M4, an adaptation of the short-barrelled M2A1. Howitzer-equipped Shermans were intended for the close support role. (*US Signal Corps*)

The M4A3E2 variant was a heavy assault tank, armed with the 75mm M3 main gun in a new heavy cast turret, with additional armour added to all of the external surfaces of the hull. The track grousers were fitted in an attempt to improve the ride. The tank was unofficially known as 'Jumbo'. (*US Signal Corps*)

Chapter Two

Sherman Production

One of the main advantages of the M4 Sherman was the relative simplicity of its design. This made it easy to manufacture and was a factor that was enthusiastically exploited, with the tank being constructed at multiple locations. By the end of 1942 five variants were in production in the USA, with the essential difference between them being largely in the choice of power unit.

The total number of Sherman gun tanks produced between 1942 and 1945 was 49,234 in the USA, and a further 188 in Canada. The largest numbers were produced at the GM Fisher Tank Arsenal at Grand Blanc, Michigan, and at the Chrysler Detroit Tank Arsenal, with totals of 11,358 and 17,947, respectively. However, during the production life of the Sherman a total of eleven plants were involved in building the tank, with dozens of sub-contractors supplying parts and major components. Several of the tank builders were more used to manufacturing railway locomotives and railcars, which of course meant that they were accustomed to handling large, heavy components, but others were able to adapt the moving production-line principle that had been so successful in the mass production of motor cars to the more onerous task of constructing large armoured fighting vehicles.

The manufacturing plants were as follows:

• The American Locomotive Company (ALCO), based in Schenectady, New York, produced 2,150 M4 variants between February and December 1943, and 150 M4A2s between September 1942 and April 1943.
• The Philadelphia-based Baldwin Locomotive Works started building M4A2 variants during October and November 1942, before switching to the M4 in January 1943. Production ceased in January 1944, by which time Baldwin had produced 1,233 M4s and just 12 M4A2s.
• Chrysler's Detroit Tank Arsenal facility was constructed during 1940/41 expressly to manufacture tanks for the US government and had a theoretical designed production rate of thirteen and a half tanks a day, with the plant operating for twenty-four hours. Production of the M4 started there on 22 July 1942 and the plant also went on to construct M4A3, M4A4 and M4A6 variants.

By June 1944 there were five assembly lines at work producing the Sherman, with total production eventually reaching 17,947 examples.

• The smallest contribution to Sherman production came from the Ohio-based Federal Machine & Welder Company, a company that was more used to manufacturing electrical equipment. The company built 540 M4A2 variants at its Warren plant between December 1942 and December 1943, averaging around fifty units a month, before switching the production facility to refurbishment work.

• The mighty Ford Motor Company built just 1,690 examples of the M4A3 at its Highland Park plant between May 1942 and September 1943 before turning to other defence projects. However, production of the GAA-III engine continued for the remaining years of the war.

• General Motors' Fisher Tank Arsenal at Grand Blanc, Michigan, constructed 11,358 Shermans between 1942 and 1945, comprising 7,508 M4A2s and 3,850 M4A3s; 254 of the latter were of the 'Jumbo' M4A3E2 assault tank variant.

• Based in a town of the same name in north-western Ohio, the Lima Locomotive Works was actually the first company to start building the Sherman, constructing the first of 1,655 examples of the M4A1 on an assembly line established for the British government at a time when Britain was buying tanks on a 'cash-and-carry' basis. Production started in February 1942 and continued to September 1943.

• The Montreal Locomotive Works, which was a subsidiary of the American Locomotive Company, constructed 188 examples of the M4A5 Grizzly between August and December 1943. These were the only examples of the Grizzly to be constructed.

• The Pacific Car & Foundry Company was based in Renton, a few miles outside Seattle, and normally manufactured railcars and wagons. Between May 1942 and November 1943 the company produced 926 M4A1 variants.

• With its headquarters in New Jersey, the Pressed Steel Car Company, which was also a manufacturer of railcars, produced a total of 8,147 Shermans, consisting of 1,000 M4s, 7,126 M4A1s and 21 M4A2s.

• In peacetime the Pullman-Standard Car Manufacturing Company was involved in manufacturing and operating luxury sleeping cars for use across the US rail network but in May 1941, having cut its teeth on the M3 medium tank, the company turned its hand to the Sherman, producing a total of 3,426 tanks, comprising 689 M4 and 2,737 M4A2 variants.

The Chrysler Corporation, the Ford Motor Company and General Motors all used plants at many other locations to produce components and sub-assemblies, and of course other companies were also involved in the supply chain. In the early years of Sherman production the availability of sufficient engines always remained a particular problem, with power units eventually produced by six different American companies.

The R-975 radial engine that had also been used in the M3, and which was used to power the M4, M4A1 and M4A5, was designed and manufactured by the Wright Aeronautical Division of the Curtiss-Wright Corporation, although most examples were actually produced under licence by the Continental Aircraft Engine Company of Mobile, Alabama. General Motors' Detroit Diesel Division produced the 6046D twin diesel power unit that had been developed for the M3A3 and was also fitted into the M4A2, while the Chrysler Corporation's Jefferson Avenue plant in Detroit was responsible for the complex thirty-cylinder A-57 multi-bank engine, also originally developed for the M3 series, and which was fitted into the M4A4. Undoubtedly the best Sherman engine was the powerful GAA-III V8 petrol engine produced by the Ford Motor Company for the M4A3. Finally, the Caterpillar Tractor Company produced the D-200A radial diesel engine that was used in the low-volume M4A6.

Transmissions were produced by Buick, the Caterpillar Tractor Company, the Detroit Tank Arsenal, the Ford Motor Company, the Iowa Transmission Company and the Reed Roller Bit Company. During the early stages of the war the transmission assemblies were purchased by the Ordnance Department and supplied as 'free issue' to the companies building the tanks, but this arrangement was eventually abandoned to allow the tank builders to make their own arrangements and to buy direct. Rubber-bushed tracks came from 'one of the leading rubber companies in Ohio'. The all-important guns, which had been developed by the US Bureau of Ordnance, were originally supplied by the various government arsenals. For example, the 75mm M2 and M3 tank guns were originally produced by Watervliet Arsenal in New York State, but the introduction of the M4 Sherman meant that the requirement for the weapon increased and other companies became involved, including the Empire Ordnance Corporation of Philadelphia, the Cowdrey Machine Works in Fitchburg, Massachusetts, and the Oldsmobile Division of General Motors.

Armour was another commodity that remained in short supply during 1942. Plans had originally been made for the Detroit Tank Arsenal to produce its own armour plate, but these were subsequently abandoned and only the Ford Motor Company and Pacific Car & Foundry used their own foundries, the former capable of producing 5,000 tons of cast armour a month. Armoured-steel castings were also produced at a variety of other locations, including American Steel Foundries, Continental Foundry & Machine Company, General Steel Castings, Pittsburgh Steel

The Toughes

Although civilian vehicle sales were severely curtailed while the USA was involved in the Second World War, Ford, like the other major manufacturers, nevertheless exploited its war production record to remind civilians that it was still in business. (*Ford Motor Company*)

Fords Ever Built!

Hard-Hitting M-4 Tanks and M-10 Tank Destroyers
Built, Armored and Powered by Ford — Praised by Army
for Performance Under Fire!

THE Ford line for 1943 features the toughest Fords ever built — technically known in the Army as 32-Ton M-4 Tanks and M-10 Tank Destroyers.

But whatever you call them they're Fords through and through . . . Armored with Ford Steel . . . Powered by a V-type Ford tank engine . . . Assembled by Ford workmen with the same skill, precision and cost-cutting ability learned in building more than 29,000,000 Ford Cars and Trucks.

Ford-made tanks *alone* are built, armored and powered by the same manufacturer! And like their peacetime predecessors, these wartime Fords have won the praise and affection of the men who use them. In the words of one high Allied commander – "The Medium Tank M-4 is the answer to a tank man's prayer!"

Of course, actual production figures are a military secret but these built-for-battle models are pouring off the lines in fleets. M-4 Tank output is far ahead of schedule. What's more, there's plenty of *extra capacity* to produce even more if required.

This is just one example of the way the men who built *your* Ford are doing today's big job. There are many more, such as the way they are producing aircraft engines, for which Ford has received the Army-Navy "E", Liberator Bombers, Gliders and Jeeps. All of these armaments are being produced in quantity. All meet the exacting quality standards demanded by the armed forces.

Measured by the most uncompromising yardsticks these wartime achievements of the Ford organization would be counted great. But we feel that *no effort short of Victory is enough.*

FORD   MOTOR   COMPANY

FORD MASS-PRODUCTION LINES DELIVER FLEETS OF WEAPONS

M-4 TANKS   •   M-10 TANK DESTROYERS

PRATT & WHITNEY AIRCRAFT ENGINES   •   JEEPS

CONSOLIDATED LIBERATOR BOMBER PLANES

TRANSPORT GLIDERS   •   UNIVERSAL CARRIERS

AMPHIBIAN JEEPS

ARMY TRUCKS   •   TANK ENGINES

TRUCK AND JEEP ENGINES

ARMOR PLATE   •   GUN MOUNTS

AIRCRAFT GENERATORS   •   TURBO-SUPERCHARGERS

RATE-OF-CLIMB INDICATORS   •   MAGNESIUM CASTINGS

This list does not include other important Victory models now in production that cannot be named due to wartime conditions.

Listen to "Watch The World Go By" featuring Earl Godwin. Every night 8:00 p.m. E.W.T. on The Blue Network.

M-10 TANK DESTROYER

FULL PRODUCTION FOR VICTORY

Foundry and Union Steel Castings. Face-hardened steel plate was supplied by American Car & Foundry, the Mosler Safe Company of Cincinnati and the Ohio-based Diebold Safe & Lock Company.

During the production life of the Sherman the US government spent almost $250 billion on building Sherman tanks, and the contracted price for each tank depended on the variant, the supplier and the date. The problem became sufficiently serious that in May 1943 the US Bureau of the Budget raised fundamental questions regarding the discrepancies between the various plants. For example, although the average 1945 price paid by the US government was $49,793, against a projected cost of $42,400, tanks produced by the Detroit Tank Arsenal consistently came in at well below this figure ... indeed, in September 1943 Chrysler told the US government that it would reduce the price of various tanks being constructed after the end of June 1944 by almost $11 million due to economies and efficiencies. At the other end of the scale, construction of the Sherman at the Fisher Tank Arsenal in 1942 alone saw General Motors invoice the US government for $256,918,000 and the company was subsequently forced to reconsider its unit price of $67,173. Federal Machine & Welder received a whopping $70,000 for each M4A2 that they constructed. Both GM and Federal Machine & Welder were working on fixed-price contracts that, in practice, turned out to be little more than estimates.

Each M4A3E2 heavy assault tank cost $56,812, and the Caterpillar-engined M4A6 was priced at $64,455, but with just seventy-five built this was not considered to be a problem.

After the tanks left the manufacturing plant, usually on flat railcars, they were generally shipped to one of the US government's tank depots where they were checked over and any necessary modifications made before the vehicle was prepared for storage and/or shipping. Tank depots were located at the New York Central Railroad workshops at Toledo in Ohio, at a redundant gun factory at Lima in Ohio, and at the Ford Motor Company plants at Chester in Pennsylvania and Richmond in California.

Of the production total of almost 50,000 Shermans, something like 19,247 examples were issued to the US Army, and a further 1,114 to the US Marine Corps. Under the arrangements laid out in the Lend-Lease Act of 1941, a total of 17,184 Shermans were supplied to Britain, some of which went to the Canadian Army and to other Commonwealth nations, including just 3 to Australia and 150 to New Zealand. A further 53 were supplied to Brazil, 4,102 went to the Soviet Union, and an estimated 812 to China; the Free French and the Free Poles also received supplies. However, this does not account for the entire production figure, falling short by a total of around 7,000.

By no means all of the tanks left the USA, and many were retained for training purposes. As D-Day approached it became clear that every available tank would be required for the invasion, and some 5,486 Shermans that had previously been assigned for training were refurbished before being shipped to Europe to be placed into storage ready to replace tanks that were lost in combat. The work, which involved cleaning and partial disassembly, followed by overhauling and modernising all of the major systems, was carried out at seven plants, and some 600 tanks a month were processed, with the cost of the work estimated to be about half the cost of building new tanks. The bulk of the work was carried out at Chrysler's Evansville Ordnance Plant and at the Quad Cities Tank Arsenal at Bettendorf, on the Iowa/Illinois border; other plants involved included the Detroit Tank Arsenal, the Federal Machine & Welder Company, the Fisher Tank Arsenal, the International Harvester Corporation, and the Montreal plant of the American Locomotive Company. A further 394 examples were refurbished at the US Army tank depots.

Between May 1942 and September 1943 the Ford Motor Company produced a total of 1,690 M4A3 Shermans on a production line installed at their Highland Park facility. (*Ford Motor Company*)

General Motors installed this massive 37-ton fixture at their Fisher Tank Arsenal at Grand Blanc, Michigan, to assist with producing the welded hull of the M4A2 Sherman. (*General Motors Corporation*)

Sherman turret castings piled up in the yard storage area at Ford's Highland Park facility. The rear counterweight is indicative of the turret for the 76mm gun. (*Ford Motor Company*)

Drilling the flange for the turret gun mounting. (*Ford Motor Company*)

Lowering the mighty Ford GAA-III V8 petrol engine into place in the M4A3; note the small working platform hooked over the edge of the engine compartment. (*Ford Motor Company*)

(*Opposite top*) Dropping the turret, complete with basket, into position. The small rotor shield for the gun indicates that this is the early M43 gun mount. (*Ford Motor Company*)

(*Opposite below*) Fitting tracks across the front sprocket; the tank has already been rolled across the lower run of track. (*Ford Motor Company*)

View of the M4A4 production line at the Chrysler Corporation's Detroit Arsenal. (*Chrysler Corporation*)

(*Opposite top*) The first M4A3 Sherman poses at the entrance to the production building at Ford's Highland Park factory. Charles E. Sorensen, who had been a major contributor to the development of the Highland Park plant in 1910, stands second from the left. (*Ford Motor Company*)

(*Opposite below*) The first M4A3 Sherman to be constructed by the Ford Motor Company was driven off the line in June 1942. (*Ford Motor Company*)

Large numbers of Shermans that had previously been assigned to training were subsequently put through a comprehensive refurbishment programme. This photograph, taken in March 1943, shows the International Harvester Corporation's works at Bettendorf, Iowa. (*US Signal Corps*)

Workers were obliged to clamber all over the tank during the assembly process and it appears that a final coat of matt green paint was sprayed over the completed vehicle at the end of the production line. (*Ford Motor Company*)

Chapter Three

The Sherman Crew

The Sherman was designed to be operated by a crew of five men, and those who wished to volunteer for training as tank crew were generally drawn from men who had already completed the standard period of basic training. In the US Army the standard five-man tank crew comprised a commander, driver, assistant driver (or co-driver/machine gunner), gunner and loader, the last-named occasionally referred to as a 'cannoneer'. The roles were identical in the British Army, but were described as commander, driver, hull gunner, turret gunner and operator.

During combat operations the men were obliged to live, eat, fight and, if possible, sleep in the tank, and this generally created a special bond between the members of the team, who often regarded one another as closer than family. The commander, gunner and loader rode in the turret, while the driver and co-driver were seated in the forward area of the hull. Access into the hull was made via two hatches in the bow, one for the driver, the other for the co-driver, and by a hatch in the turret roof; an additional hatch was provided in the turret roof for the loader in late 1943 and kits were devised to enable this modification to be applied to existing vehicles. Each man had a designated seat inside the hull. The driver's seat and the co-driver's seat were similar, with removable backs, and with lever-adjustment for reach and height; the other three seats were adjustable for height only. Restraining belts were provided to prevent the crewmen being thrown around the interior during off-road operations, and various internal surfaces in the hull were padded for safety.

While the standard five-man crew was ideal, a shortage of trained men often meant that it was not uncommon for tanks to go into battle with as few as three crew members, which meant that the commander was obliged to double as the loader. The Sherman Firefly was routinely operated by four men, since the size of the gun breech meant that space inside the fighting compartment was at a premium.

The roles of the crew require some explanation.

As the name suggests, the commander was the senior crew member; in the US Army the commander of a platoon command tank generally held the rank of lieutenant, while other tanks of the platoon were usually commanded by a sergeant. The commander's role was to identify likely targets, and to choose the appropriate form of ammunition to eliminate the particular threat. It was also part of his role to instruct the gunner, and to co-ordinate the actions of his tank with others in his platoon or troop.

The gunner, who was usually a corporal, took his orders from the commander and was responsible for laying the main gun onto the target, and for firing it via the footswitch. The gunner was also responsible for the co-axial machine gun, and would frequently fire this before the main gun as a means of verifying that the target had been correctly identified.

The loader was considered to be unskilled and was usually a private. His role was to take the appropriate ammunition from the racks as instructed by the commander, or from the floor where it might have been placed ready for an engagement, and to push the round hard into the breech; this would release the latch that allowed the spring-loaded breech to close. At the same time the loader would kick the gunner's shin to indicate that the gun was ready to fire. It was normal practice for only the lead tank in a column to travel with the main gun loaded, which meant that the loader was required to open the breech for the first round of any engagement. After a round was fired, the breech was automatically opened and the spent cartridge ejected. When conditions permitted, the loader was also tasked with disposing of spent cartridges manually through the roof hatch or the turret pistol port, and with aiding the commander in the use of the radio.

The role of the co-driver/machine gunner — sometimes referred to as the 'bow gunner' or BOG — was to fire the hull-mounted machine gun. Curiously, despite the description of the role, he had no driving responsibilities!

Finally, the driver's role seems obvious but, as well as being responsible for moving the tank from one location to another, his role included ensuring that the tank was manoeuvred into an appropriate firing position, exploiting whatever cover was available. The driver normally rode with his head out of the hatch, and a folding weatherproof hood and windscreen was provided to protect him against dust and inclement weather. The driving controls included conventional pedals for the throttle and clutch, together with a pair of spring-loaded braking levers that were used to make steering corrections. The official training manual suggested that the driver should keep his hands away from the steering levers unless he wanted to turn the tank, but most drivers found this very unnatural and preferred to hold the levers lightly at all times. The job was very demanding: without power assistance on the clutch-withdrawal mechanism, the steering levers or the gear shift, driving the tank was hard work and could become very tiring over long periods.

Even when the guns were not being fired, the inside of a Sherman was an extraordinarily noisy environment, with the roar of the engine behind, the whining of the transmission and the incessant clatter of the tracks, and the crew communicated with one another via an internal intercom system. Each crew member wore a throat microphone and a pair of headphones, the latter incorporated in the leather tanker's helmet, which, incidentally, was often worn in conjunction with a steel helmet by means of a bit of nifty 'field modification'. The commander was also provided with a hand-held microphone, and a handset on the rear of the hull allowed the crew to communicate with infantrymen outside the tank.

The entrance hatches in the turret and in the forward area of the hull doubled as escape hatches, and there was an additional emergency hatch provided in the floor. If necessary, the order to evacuate would be given by the commander, who would be the first to exit, simply because he was closest to the hatch and no one could get past him.

Of course, the duties of the crew extended beyond simply fighting, and the proper functioning of the various systems in the tank were essential to the crew's chances of surviving. At the beginning and end of each day, and during breaks in fighting or at unscheduled stops, the men were also required to conduct various simple maintenance tasks to ensure that the tank remained in fighting condition. In the British Army at least, the tasks were set out in the 'Crew Duty Card' and the troop commander was required to sign record sheets on a weekly basis to confirm that the tasks had been satisfactorily completed, and the squadron commander was similarly required to sign once a month.

To sum up, volunteering for tank crew was no picnic. While injury rates among tank crew were generally lower than those experienced by infantry, those injuries that were sustained tended to be of greater (up to 50 per cent) severity and mortality, as well as there being an increased incidence of burns and traumatic amputations. A US 12th Army Group report stated that tank-crew casualties averaged one man killed and one man wounded when a Sherman was knocked out, while a study carried out by the US 1st Army concluded that, of tank crew casualties, the ratio was roughly one man killed to every three wounded.

The Sherman was designed to be operated by a crew of five – commander, driver, assistant driver (or co-driver/machine gunner), gunner and loader. These men are wearing the early US Army M1930 tank crew composition helmet. (*US Signal Corps*)

(*Opposite top*) A shortage of trained men often meant that tanks were put into battle with just three or four crew members; in this situation the commander was obliged to double as the loader. (*US Signal Corps*)

(*Opposite below*) The driver's position, showing the twin steering levers, the instrument panel and the driver's periscope. (*Ford Motor Company*)

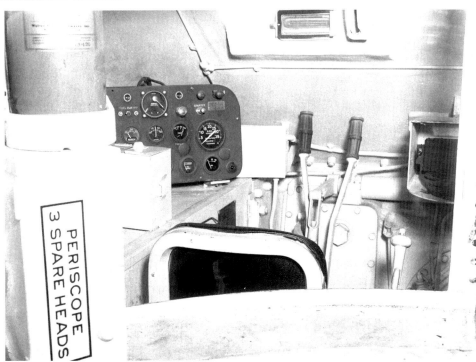

PERISCOPE
3 SPARE HEADS

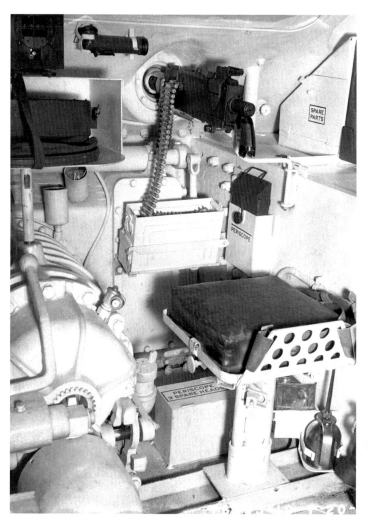

The workplace for the assistant driver (or co-driver/machine gunner) showing the bow machine gun. Note the huge transmission casting that separates the driver and co-driver. (*Ford Motor Company*)

A US Marine Corps five-man crew photographed in Saipan, July 1944. (*US Signal Corps*)

A view of the turret basket, showing the gunner's seat (on the left). The commander's seat is hidden behind the backrest of the gunner's seat, but the loader's seat can be seen behind that; there is an alternative seat for the commander on the right. (*Ford Motor Company*)

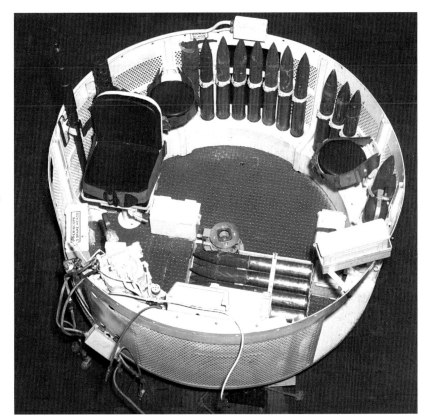

From 1942 US tank crews wore one-piece herringbone twill coveralls, often with a zipped windcheater jacket. These men are seated on a Sherman that has had the turret removed to create an armoured carrier. (*Warehouse Collection*)

The five-man crew of this British Army Sherman M4A4 Firefly pose happily with a crowd of liberated Dutch or Belgian children. (*Warehouse Collection*)

Although he is hard to spot among the crowd of precariously seated but cheerful combat troops, the commander is riding with the cupola hatch open. The loader and co-driver hatches are also open. (*Warehouse Collection*)

A telephone handset at the rear of the tank allowed infantry to communicate with the crew. Despite the infantrymen apparently using the tank as a shield, the fact that the turret hatches are open suggests that the photographed is posed. (*US Signal Corps*)

Chapter Four

The Sherman in Combat

Although it could be built in large numbers relatively cheaply, and was considered both reliable and easy to drive, in truth the Sherman was no great shakes as a fighting vehicle. Even when it was introduced in 1942, it could scarcely have been described as 'state-of-the-art' and, worse still, the lack of real development in terms of firepower and protection meant that by mid-1943 it was becoming increasingly obsolescent. Indeed, by the later stages of the war it was arguably both out-gunned and out-armoured by the heavier German machines. And as if this were not enough, the narrow tracks of all but the later models increased ground pressure and restricted its manoeuvrability, particularly in difficult conditions, a drawback that was partially overcome by the use of duck-bill grousers to extend the width of the tracks. And the rubber tracks, so admired by the Germans for their 'soft' ride, offered very little traction in soft terrain. On the plus side, it did at least possess a reasonable turn of speed and in many situations was perfectly capable of advancing on its own tracks, albeit requiring the constant attention of the Ordnance repair teams.

It was only by virtue of the large numbers that could be thrown into battle, and the sheer doggedness of the Allied crews, that the Sherman was able to prevail. It was not until the Anglo-American Sherman Firefly appeared in mid-1944, with its powerful 17-pounder (76.2mm) anti-tank gun, that the Allies at last had a tank that was able to match the German *Tiger* and *Panther* on a more-or-less equal footing ... but it might well have been a different story altogether had the Germans been able to learn the lessons of mass production from the Americans. Nevertheless, for most of the war the Sherman was the best all-round tank available to the Western Allies – and it was certainly the best in 1942. Both the US Army and the Marine Corps were re-equipped with Shermans to replace their M3 mediums, while the British and Commonwealth Armies continued to receive supplies of the Sherman throughout the war to supplement the often unreliable tanks supplied by their domestic factories.

The Sherman was probably a better all-round tank than most of the British tanks of that period of the war, and one very distinct advantage was the ability of the dual-purpose 75mm and 76mm guns to fire all types of ammunition, including high-explosive, as well as solid, ballistic-capped and hyper-velocity armour-piercing rounds. High-explosive rounds were frequently fired indirectly (ie, without the gunner having sight of the target) to deal with enemy rearguards, while the armour-piercing rounds were used against enemy armour. It is also worth noting that the use of an admittedly somewhat primitive single-plane hydraulic gyro-stabiliser on the gun mount, allowing the Sherman to fire on the move, gave it something of an advantage over the German tanks of the period that lacked such equipment. In truth, though, the likelihood of achieving a hit on the move was low and it was suggested in official documentation that firing on the move should only be done in an emergency ... and then only if the range was less than 600yd.

The Sherman saw its first action in the Middle East, where some 318 M4A1 and M4A2 variants (Sherman II and III), many taken from US Army training facilities, were pitched against Rommel's *Panzers* by units of Montgomery's British Eighth Army during the second battle of El Alamein in October/November 1942. Rommel's German forces had 249 tanks at their disposal, consisting of a mixture of *Panzer IIs*, armed with a 20mm gun, *Panzer IIIs*, including variants with both the long (L/60) and short (L/42) 50mm gun, and *Panzer IVs*, with both the long (L/43) and short (L/24) 75mm guns. On paper, the German 50mm and 75mm guns both had the edge in penetration power when compared to the Sherman's 75mm gun, but by engaging at a range of 2,000yd the Shermans managed to knock out a number of enemy tanks and forced the demoralised Germans to withdraw. However, one can only presume that the Germans were taken somewhat by surprise by their first encounter with the Sherman, having become used to the British Crusader with its decidedly inferior 2-pounder (40mm) gun. Even the 6-pounder (57mm) gun of the later Crusader III, which was also fielded in Egypt, was scarcely a match for the German 50mm, let alone the 75mm.

But there was no doubt that the Sherman was considerably better than the M3 Lee/Grant, and by the end of 1942 the US 2nd Armored Division had replaced all of the earlier tanks. In November 1942 the Shermans were key to the success of 'Operation Torch' – the Anglo-American invasion of French North Africa, where the Allies came up against outdated French tanks and reputedly had a 9:1 superiority in terms of armour. However, whilst the Sherman might have been adequate for confrontations with older French tanks, and with the *Panzer III* and *IV*, it was sadly lacking when confronted by the German *Panther* and *Tiger* tanks against which it was required to fight in the later years of the war, and this was a lesson that the Germans quickly learned.

Nevertheless, Shermans played a crucial role in the D-Day landings, where the 'funnies' really came into their own, and in the subsequent breakout from the Normandy region and the advance through France and the Low Countries into Germany.

On D-Day itself amphibious DD (duplex drive) Shermans were issued to eight tank battalions of American, British and Canadian forces. Four or five vehicles were carried in a 'landing craft, tank' (LCT) to within 2 miles or so of the shore, where they were launched into the sea. Providing the sea was relatively calm, the tanks were able to 'swim' successfully to the shore, where the theory was that they would be able to overpower the German defences. However, for a variety of reasons many were lost prematurely, most notably at Omaha beach, where none of the tanks that were launched managed to reach the shore. DD Shermans were also used, more successfully, during the Rhine crossing.

Sherman Crab flail tanks were enormously useful in dealing with German minefields, particularly on the Normandy beaches. On the British invasion beaches, for example, Crabs were operated by the Lothian and Border Horse, the 22nd Dragoons and the Westminster Dragoons, as part of the 79th Armoured Division. The Crabs were generally operated in groups of five, with three tanks moving forward in echelon formation clearing a broad path through the minefield, while the other two would provide fire support, as well as being able to replace any of the three leaders should they become disabled. On D-Day, for example, Sherman Crabs flailed their way up Gold (Arromanches-les-Bains) and Juno (Courselles) beaches, exploding mines both above and below the waterline; the operation was not without danger and Crabs were frequently disabled by mines that had not been set off by the chains. Where an exploding mine created a crater large enough to present a hazard, a Bullshorn plough was used to fill it in.

Following the success of the Normandy landings, Allied tanks almost always outnumbered those of the *Wehrmacht*, although this was not always sufficient to ensure an easy ride. The Germans built fewer than 6,000 *Panthers*, and there were scarcely 1,400 *Tigers* and 500 *Königstigers* ... but on average it took between six and fifteen Shermans to destroy one *Tiger*, and this disparity in performance between the Allied and German tanks often led to shortages of Shermans during the heavy fighting in the Normandy *bocage* country, where it proved difficult and hazardous for the Allied tank crews to break through the dense hedgerows and get their tanks off the roads. During June, July and August 1944 the US 1st Army alone lost 666 of its 2,890 medium tanks. It was not until a US Army Staff Sergeant named Curtis G. Culin developed a fabricated steel device designed to be attached to the front of the hull to uproot hedgerows that any real progress was made. The device, which was often fabricated from old German beach defences, was fitted to both M3/M5 Stuart light tanks and to Shermans, and was most effective during 'Operation Cobra', the breakout from Normandy. Tanks that were so equipped were described as either Sherman Rhinoceros or Sherman Prong ... but it does make you wonder how the German tanks fared when faced with the same obstacles.

When the 76mm gun was introduced in 1943, the US Army had planned that one-third of the tanks in a unit would be armed with the larger gun, the remainder retaining the 75mm. However, notwithstanding the difficulties of getting tanks through the tough hedgerows of the *bocage* country, the nature of the fighting in Normandy also proved that the 75mm gun was totally inadequate against the German *Tiger* and *Panther*, and there are reports of Allied tank crews resorting to ramming German tanks in an effort to disable them. This created pressure for more 76mm gun tanks and by the early summer of 1944 the number of Shermans in US Army units that were equipped with the 76mm gun was closer to 50 per cent ... and if some contemporary reports are to be believed, there were those US commanders who would have liked all of their Shermans to be armed with the British OQF 17-pounder (76.2mm) gun!

Once the Allies had broken out of the Normandy fields, the fast-moving columns of tanks advancing across France were supported by fighter-bombers in the air. This tended to discourage one-on-one tank action and exploited the advantages of the Sherman by creating ideal conditions for the fast-moving columns of Allied armour.

In many cases the Shermans were able to advance under their own power but there were occasions where the commanders on the ground judged that transporters were required. For this role the US Army favoured the M26 Pacific TR-1 'Dragon Wagon' tractor, a massive 45-ton prime mover, produced in armoured and soft-skin form, and designed to be used with a Fruehauf M15 semi-trailer: the complete train was described as 'truck-trailer, 45-ton, tank transporter, M25'. Alternatively, the 'truck-trailer, 45-ton, tank transporter, M19' might have been used, consisting of the Diamond T Model 980 or 981 tractor, in combination with a 45-ton drawbar trailer. The British Army used either the same type of Diamond T tractor, generally with a 40-ton British trailer, or the ageing Scammell Pioneer TRMU30 tractor, together with its dedicated TRCU30 semi-trailer. With a nominal maximum load rating of 30 tons, the Pioneer was loaded to its limit with a combat-ready Sherman.

British and US Army Shermans also saw action in Belgium – where Shermans were pitched head-to-head against German *Panthers* in the Ardennes – in France, Germany, Italy, the Netherlands, North Africa and Sicily.

The *Wehrmacht* was also not averse to fielding captured Shermans, particularly after the invasion of Normandy. The first Sherman had been captured in Tunisia back in 1943 and was apparently transported back to Berlin 'under its own power' where it was examined by German engineers, with admiration expressed for details such as the cast armour and rubber-faced tracks. Many German units established a 'captured tank unit' and equipped it with Shermans, which they described as the *Panzerkampfwagen M4-748*, and even a Firefly was captured and used against the Allies. Presumably any tank is better than no tank at all, but one has to wonder what the German crews made of these vehicles.

The Canadian-built M4A5 Grizzlies were mostly restricted to training, but there is some evidence that the type also saw service with the 5th Canadian Armoured Division in north-west Europe. (*Warehouse Collection*)

But Allied tank crews were always concerned at the Sherman's lack of armour and in the US Army it became fairly common practice to add what might be described as 'field expedient *appliqué* armour' to the glacis plate, the turret and the flanks of the tank in an attempt (generally ineffective) at improving the resistance to armour-piercing rounds and the dreaded *Panzerfaust* anti-tank grenade. Those with access to workshop facilities frequently welded in place additional armour that had been cut from the hulls of scrap tanks, but other materials commonly employed included railway sleepers, sandbags, concrete, rocks, track links, logs and spare bogie wheels.

While all of this was going on in the 'real world', the US War Department was keen to reassure the public that 'US tanks were superior to anything the enemy could produce' ... and even the great George Patton himself was on record as saying that 'in mechanical endurance and ease of maintenance our tanks are infinitely superior to any other'. But it was what he didn't say that gave the game away, and the truth was that secret reports coming back from the front told a very different story. Complaints ranged from the lack of good binoculars for the commander to the inferiority of both the main gun and the level of armoured protection. Questions began to be asked in the States, with many critics wondering why the USA was unable to produce better tanks than Germany, and asking why the USA did not produce a heavy tank that was capable of standing up to the German *Tiger*. True, the Sherman had the advantage of numbers, it was reliable and provided an excellent range of action, but the Allied tank crews were frequently forced to consider how the Sherman might best be deployed tactically against the better-armoured enemy rather than being able to take on the Germans on equal terms. This approach by attrition was a hard way to win a war and, in the words of General Omar Bradley, 'this willingness to expend Shermans offered little comfort to the crews who were forced to expend themselves as well'. No wonder the Sherman was often described as a 'purple heart box'.

All Sherman crews lived in constant fear of unexpectedly encountering a *Tiger*, but even when this was not the case, fighting against any enemy tank in a Sherman must have been hot, exhausting and, if there had been time to think about what was going on, frightening. Hot, spent shell cases would pile up on the floor of the turret basket, eventually to be ejected manually through the roof hatch or the turret pistol port, and despite the roof extractor fans the interior would fill with the acrid smell of cordite. Enemy machine-gun fire would rattle against the exterior of the hull. A direct hit from either an anti-tank round or a *Panzerfaust* which failed to penetrate the armour would create 'a terrific thud' or 'a hell of a crack', and make the tank rock on its springs. There would be localised heating of the hull at the point of impact as the kinetic energy of the incoming round was converted to heat energy, and this would inevitably be accompanied by spalling of hot particles of metal from the inner face, as well as showers of dust and loose material from inside the hull. The crew would, inevitably, be left wondering whether or not the next round might penetrate the armour and one can only imagine the tension and the conditions inside the tank.

The effect of landmines was similarly devastating, rocking the tank on its suspension and often disabling it by blowing off a wheel station or by breaking the tracks ... thus making the tank a sitting-duck target for any enemy armour.

At close range the larger German guns had the capacity to send an armour-piercing projectile right through the hull of the Sherman, creating untold mayhem inside the fighting compartment. This would result in a shower of molten metal particles inside, which, aside from killing or seriously injuring crew members, could short out electrical equipment and start a devastating fire. In the words of one tank crewman, 'a German "88" sure makes quick work [*of a tank hull*] ... they go through them just like they were a piece of paper'. There are even tales of two Shermans being disabled with a single shot, the round passing through one hull before penetrating the tank next to it.

Fire was an ever-present threat. Despite the adoption of the wet ammunition storage system, Shermans still exhibited an unfortunate tendency to go up in flames, leading to the Germans dubbing the vehicles 'Tommy Cookers'; US troops frequently referred to the Sherman as a 'Ronson'. At first it was believed that it was the use of petrol as a fuel that made the Shermans so prone to 'brewing-up', but it was later proved that the large majority of tank fires were the result of an explosion of the ammunition in unprotected bins. Although the Sherman was equipped with a fire-extinguishing system, consisting of two fixed 10lb fire-extinguishers in the engine compartment designed to be operated by the driver or from outside the tank, and two 4lb portable extinguishers in the driver's compartment and in the turret, even the fixed system had to be operated manually and there wasn't always time to trigger it. Any fire would quickly become established and burn out of control, particularly if the cupola or any of the hatches were open. Internal explosions would frequently destroy the hull or dislodge the turret, and a burned-out tank was generally considered to be fit only for scrap since the heat of the fire would destroy the hardness of the armour.

If a tank was hit and rendered unfit for continued service, the crew were often forced to evacuate over the bodies of their dead or seriously injured comrades; if the tank was not badly damaged, they were often required, when conditions allowed, to clean the interior of the hull to make the vehicle ready for further use. Tanks that were severely damaged but not destroyed were hauled away for assessment and repair. Many were put back into service following workshop repairs, but, not surprisingly, crews were not at all happy at being obliged to take on a tank that had been breached, no matter how well it had been repaired.

And it wasn't necessarily the case that the Sherman crews were able to give as good as they got. There are anecdotal stories of rounds fired by Shermans simply 'bouncing off' the armour of the *Tiger* or *Panther*, and 'scratching the paint' but causing little real damage. One tank commander reported that his crew fired 'twenty-five or more rounds' at a particular German tank without managing to disable it. A German tank could be taken out by means of a lucky shot that either broke a track, although of course this had no effect on the operation of the gun, or jammed the turret; indeed, the *Tiger* that currently resides in the Tank Museum was captured after its crew abandoned it because the turret had been jammed, albeit the disabling shot was fired by a Churchill. It was only the appearance of the Anglo-American Sherman Firefly that gave Allied tank crews a real chance of taking out one of the German heavy tanks in head-to-head combat. Indeed, writing after the end of the conflict Major-General Sir Campbell Clarke observed that the 'Firefly ... was able to outpace, out-manoeuvre and outshoot ... the German Tiger'.

Things were different in the Pacific and Far East campaigns, where the Sherman was usually deployed against Japanese infantry positions, and the Japanese Imperial Forces quickly came to understand the superiority of the vehicle compared to their own tanks. The US Marines often equipped their Shermans with, sometimes improvised, wading equipment to facilitate beach landings as they fought their way across the Pacific islands. Although there were some engagements in open territory, there were no large-scale tank-on-tank battles in the Pacific theatre, and the Marines generally fought in close combat, favouring high-explosive rounds to deal with Japanese defensive positions and with the hatches closed to counter the ever-present threat of snipers. M4A2s were favoured because the diesel fuel was felt to be less likely to result in a fire if a tank was hit, but when the production of this variant came to an end in May 1944 the Marines switched to the Ford-engined M4A3. Modifications unique to this theatre included the addition of side-skirts to prevent satchel charges being thrown under the hull, rows of nails or 'bird cages' welded around the hatch openings to provide a stand-off, which was also a response to the widespread use of satchel charges, and the addition of sand-coated corrugated-steel roofing sheets and timber or timber/concrete cladding to the hull to discourage the use of magnetic mines, and to reduce the vulnerability of the Sherman to the Japanese 47mm anti-tank rounds. The shortcomings of the Sherman's narrow tracks also became more than apparent on Iwo Jima, where the volcanic pumice soil resulted in tanks getting bogged down and sometimes actually breaking tracks. Anti-tank mines, including various types of improvised device, remained an ever-present threat and resulted in the largest number of battle casualties among the Marines' Shermans.

As regards tank-on-tank action, the Sherman was considerably superior to the

The weakest areas of armoured protection on the Sherman are apparent in the floor, and cresting a ridge in this way makes the tank very vulnerable to enemy fire. (*Ford Motor Company*)

relatively light Japanese Type 95 HA-GO and KYU-GO tanks that were equipped with nothing more powerful than a 37mm gun, and were protected by just 17mm of armour. As an example of the disparity between the tanks of the opposing sides, on Kwajalein Atoll US forces captured a Japanese Type 94 light tank and loaded it, complete, across the engine deck of an M4A2 before transporting it back to Hawaii as a souvenir. The up-gunned versions of the medium Type 97 CHI-HA or the CHI-NU tank, the former generally considered to be among the best Japanese tanks of the period, were perhaps another matter, but the Sherman was generally able to prevail.

The Chinese successfully deployed 100 Shermans against Japanese forces during 1943 and 1944, and the Red Army favoured the Sherman over the larger but better protected T-34 in certain situations, particularly street fighting, even going so far as to fit the 76.2mm F-34 gun of the T-34 to some examples, which were designated M4M.

However, for all its shortcomings – and there were plenty – the Sherman undoubtedly helped to turn the tide of the war. There is little doubt, however, that by 1945 tank technology had moved on considerably, leaving the Sherman behind.

At the end of the war the US Army reputedly possessed around 10,000 Shermans, and the favoured variant for continued service was the M4A3E8 – the so-called 'Easy Eight'. By 1950 the number available had been reduced to 3,202, but many of these were unserviceable. From 1950 US Army Shermans were pressed into action during the Korean War, where they fought alongside the M26 Pershing and M46 Patton. Eventually, some 680 'Easy Eights' were deployed in Korea, often engaging the late production Soviet T-34 tanks with their 85mm guns, as well as proving fire support for infantry. In late 1950 US tanks took part in more than 100 tank-on-tank engagements in Korea; although on paper the T-34 and the Sherman were more-or-less evenly matched, the Sherman's superior sighting and fire-control equipment, and better-trained crews, normally ensured that it would prevail, particularly when the US crews had access to hyper-velocity armour-piercing (HVAP) rounds. When compared to the heavier M26, the Sherman was considered to be more reliable and easier to maintain.

After the Korean War ended, US Army Shermans were relegated to a training role, before finally being declared obsolete in 1956. Its replacements were the M26 Pershing, which had been developed in the closing years of the Second World War, and the M46 Patton, dating from 1947/48.

During 1945/46 Britain had returned all its unwanted Sherman gun tanks to the USA in order to reduce the nation's liability for Lend-Lease repayments, and had replaced them with the Centurion, which, had its development been completed in time, would certainly have been the best Allied tank of the Second World War. A few specialised Sherman types remained in service into the post-war years, most notably the beach armoured recovery vehicle (BARV). Similarly Canada abandoned all of its Shermans in Europe, leaving them with the Dutch and Belgian Armies; many of the M4A5 Grizzlies eventually ended up in Portugal. That wasn't the end of the story for Shermans in Canada, however, because in 1946 300 M4A2 HVSS Shermans equipped with the 76mm gun were purchased and were retained into the mid-1950s, when they were replaced with British-built Centurions. The Soviet Union also returned some of the Lend-Lease Shermans that they had received back in the early days of the war, although a few of those that were retained were converted to railway tractors!

While the machine might have been considered obsolete by the West by the mid-1950s, many remaining ex-US Army and other Shermans were subsequently transferred to other friendly nations where they enjoyed a second lease of life. Alongside its use by the Western Allies – Britain, Canada, the Soviet Union and the United States – during the Second World War, the Sherman went on to see service with more than thirty nations. The full list of those deploying the Sherman includes Argentina, Australia, Brazil, Chile, (People's Republic of) China, Cuba, Denmark, Egypt, France, India, Iran, Israel, Italy, Japan, Lebanon, Netherlands, New Zealand, Nicaragua, Pakistan, Paraguay, Peru, Philippines, Poland, Portugal, Republic of China (Taiwan), Saudi Arabia, South Africa, South Korea, Syria, Turkey and Yugoslavia. Quite a roll call!

The Israeli Defence Force (IDF) was probably the largest post-war user of the Sherman, with a total of 700 examples acquired from various sources, initially from Britain, but with some even coming from scrapyards. A number were also captured from neighbouring Arab states during the Arab–Israeli Wars of 1956, 1967 and 1973–74.

As regards the Sherman's role in post-war conflicts, the hardening of the ideological split between East and West meant that many Shermans went into action *against* the Soviet T-34. Despite obvious disparities in armour and technology, the two tanks were surprisingly well matched. Shermans also fought during the Chinese and Greek Civil Wars, and in the First Indo-China War, and were used by both sides in the Indo–Pakistan War of 1965, with the Egyptian Army in Suez, in Cuba on the side of the Batista government, and in Nicaragua during the Sandinista Revolution of 1978–79. The last action in which Shermans were used in anger was probably the Lebanese Civil War, which lasted from 1975 to 1990.

In the immediate post-war years there was little demand for ageing tanks outside of the military and many were cut up for scrap. However, surprisingly, a few old Shermans were converted into agricultural tractors, where, stripped of all unnecessary weight, they proved to be very adept at tasks such as logging and heavy ploughing, as well as acting as road crawlers and prime movers for a variety of applications. And bearing in mind that almost 50,000 examples were constructed, it should be no surprise that possibly hundreds have survived in museums around the world, and as static monuments at various strategic sites, particularly in France.

What's more, the relatively low cost of surplus Shermans back in the 1980s means that there are also more than a few in private hands.

What could be more iconic … an M4 Sherman followed by the ubiquitous Jeep. Note the additional armour protecting the driver and co-driver's positions and the *appliqué* panel on the hull side protecting the ammunition stowage areas. (*Warehouse Collection*)

(*Opposite top*) Dated March 1945, this photograph shows a Sherman being used to drag a burning German – although in this case it's a French-built Citroën – vehicle clear of the road. The hatches are open so the crew obviously do not feel they are in any danger. (*US Signal Corps*)

(*Opposite below*) A cast-hull M4A1 disembarking from an American LST (landing ship, tank) during a landing manoeuvre *en route* to North Africa in October 1943. (*US Navy*)

A Ford-built M4A3 showing its paces. While many criticisms could be levelled at the Sherman, including being under-gunned and under-protected, it was easy to drive and possessed a reasonable turn of speed. (*Ford Motor Company*)

(*Opposite top*) Shermans of the Free French being prepared for combat. After the Second World War the Sherman went on to see service with more than thirty nations. (*US Signal Corps*)

(*Opposite below*) Photographed on 24 August 1944, some 6 miles south of Paris, these Shermans of the French 2nd Armoured Division are rolling through the town of Sceaux. At the time there was still some street fighting in the outskirts of the French capital. (*US Signal Corps*)

The chalked legend tells a sad but all too common story. Three Free French soldiers died when this Sherman brewed up as a result of enemy fire. The photograph was taken at the Gare des Invalides in Paris. (*Warehouse Collection*)

A US Army M7 Priest 105mm gun motor carriage (self-propelled gun) rolling through Carentan. The Priest was originally based on the chassis of the M3 medium tank but when production of this ceased, the M4 was used. (*US Signal Corps*)

During the Battle of the Bulge in the winter of 1944/45 the US Shermans, which were at a grave disadvantage when facing heavy German tanks, were hastily daubed with white paint to provide camouflage in the snow. (*Warehouse Collection*)

A Free French Sherman advancing across a floating pontoon bridge erected across the Rhine. (*US Signal Corps*)

A knocked-out British Army 75mm Sherman abandoned in a ditch. The censor has obliterated the unit markings that were partly visible on the right-hand side of the glacis plate. (*Tank Museum*)

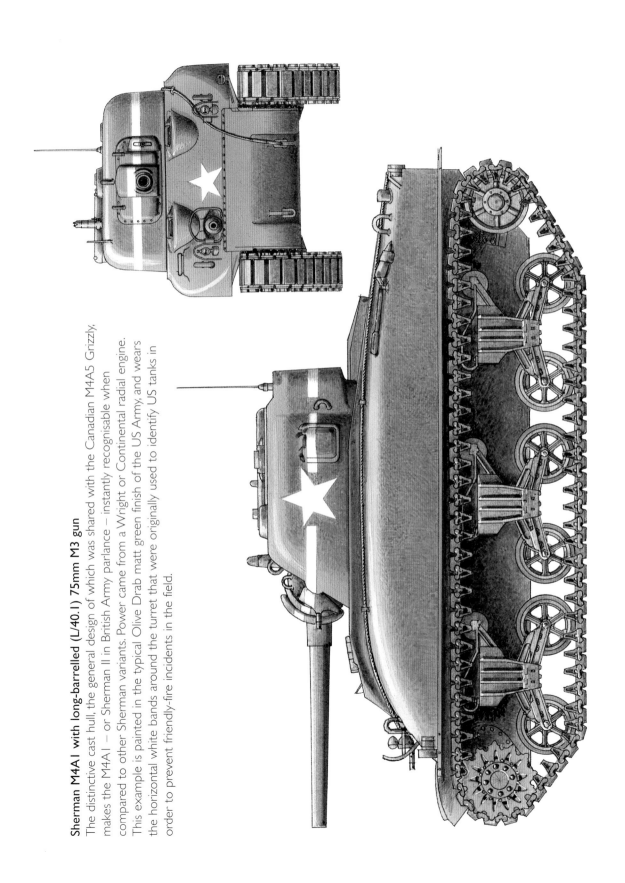

Sherman M4A1 with long-barrelled (L/40.1) 75mm M3 gun

The distinctive cast hull, the general design of which was shared with the Canadian M4A5 Grizzly, makes the M4A1 – or Sherman II in British Army parlance – instantly recognisable when compared to other Sherman variants. Power came from a Wright or Continental radial engine. This example is painted in the typical Olive Drab matt green finish of the US Army, and wears the horizontal white bands around the turret that were originally used to identify US tanks in order to prevent friendly-fire incidents in the field.

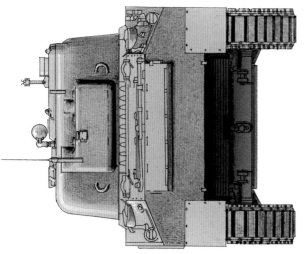

Sherman M4A2 with long-barrelled (L/40.1) 75mm M3 gun

Described by the British as the Sherman III, the M4A2 was powered by twin General Motors six-cylinder diesel engines, and featured a welded hull. This example has the wider rotor shield to the main gun that was adopted in October 1942.

Although wearing nothing more than its factory finish of matt green, the registration number – T146943 – identifies this tank as being destined for the British Army. Following issue to a unit, the tank would also receive formation and tactical markings indicating the arm of service, division and regiment, as well as the distinctive white star and circle markings that were used by all the Allied armies after about 1942 as an air recognition symbol.

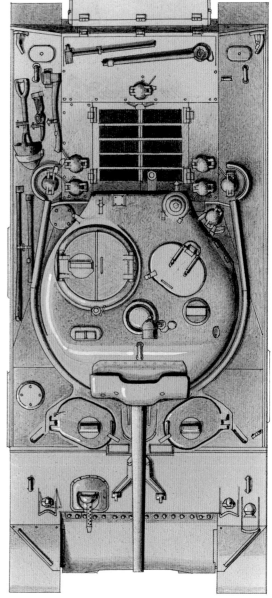

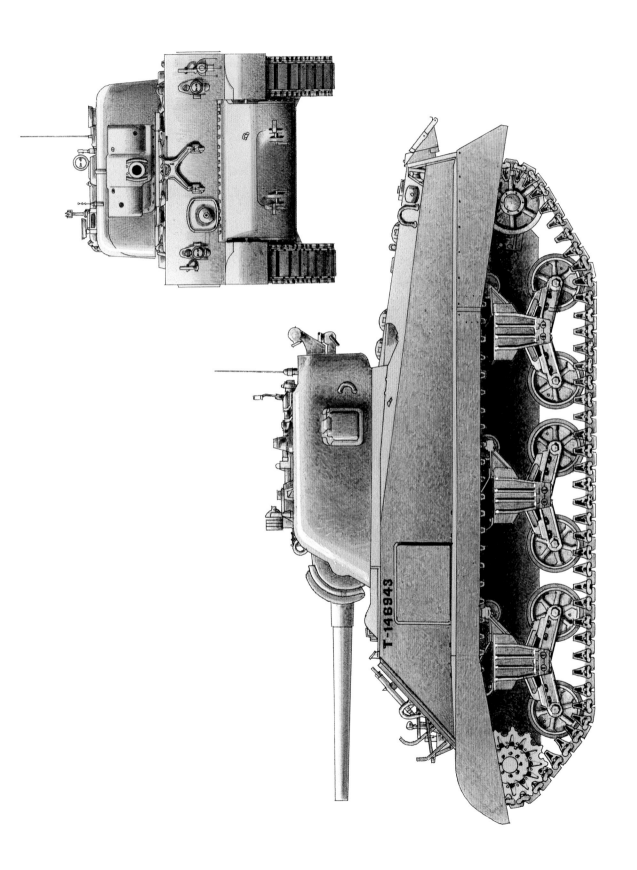

Sherman M4A3E8 with 76mm gun

The wide-tracked Ford-engined M4A3E8 – colloquially described by GIs as the 'Easy Eight' – was fitted with the improved horizontal volute suspension system (HVSS), and was the Sherman variant most favoured by the US Army during the Second World War, going on to also see service in Korea. It was described by the British Army as the Sherman IVAY, although few were deployed outside the US Army.

This example has been fitted with racks that allow sandbags to be carried on the outside of the hull to improve protection. The additional weight will have done little to help the tank's automotive performance. Note the later horizontal volute spring suspension (HVSS) and wider T66 tracks that gave a much-improved ride. The sandbags have covered all of the areas used by the US Army for tactical markings, forcing these to be moved to the barrel. The figure '14' followed by a triangle marking indicates the 14th Armored Division, while the other figures indicate the 25th Tank Battalion, with this tank the seventeenth vehicle in the order of march.

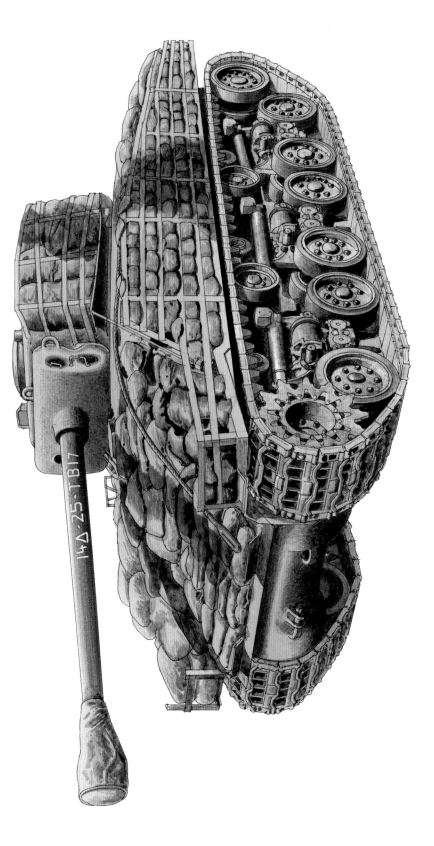

Sherman M4E5 with 105mm gun

Based on the standard M4 welded hull, the M4E5 was a prototype for an artillery support variant of the Sherman using a 105mm howitzer mounted on its side in a modified turret. The tank was put into production in both M4 and M4A2 form.

The tank shown here, belonging to the US Army 15th Armored Division, has received a hasty coat of white paint over the standard Olive Drab to camouflage it in snow. Note how the white paint has worn off sharp edges and has been deliberately removed from around the markings.

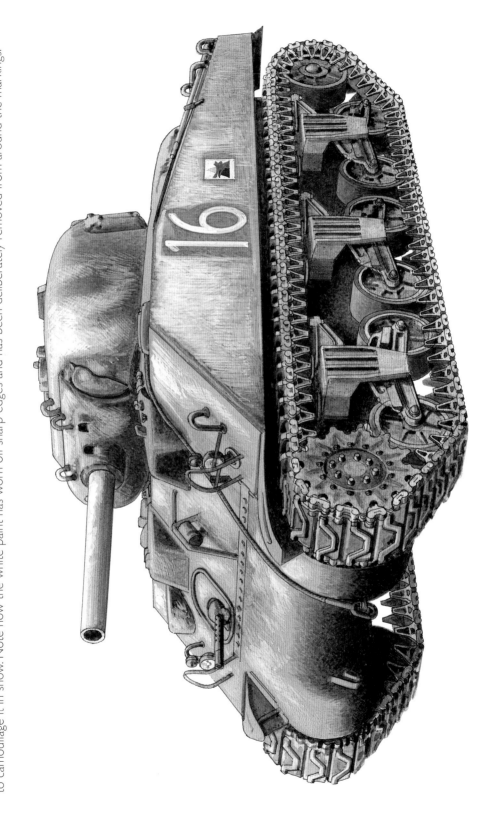

Sherman M4A2E8 with 76mm gun

Powered by twin General Motors diesel engines, and fitted with wide tracks and horizontal volute spring suspension, this M4A2E8 – Sherman IIIAY – was sent to Britain for evaluation, and carries the British registration number T-224875. The markings above the registration number on the hull sides state, 'This vehicle is filled with anti-freeze 1/3 2/3 and must not be drained.' The tank forms part of the collection of the Tank Museum and can often be seen running.

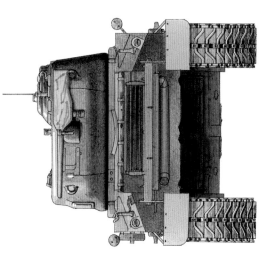

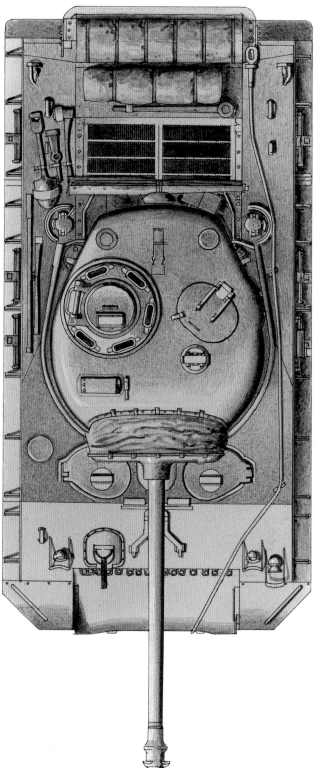

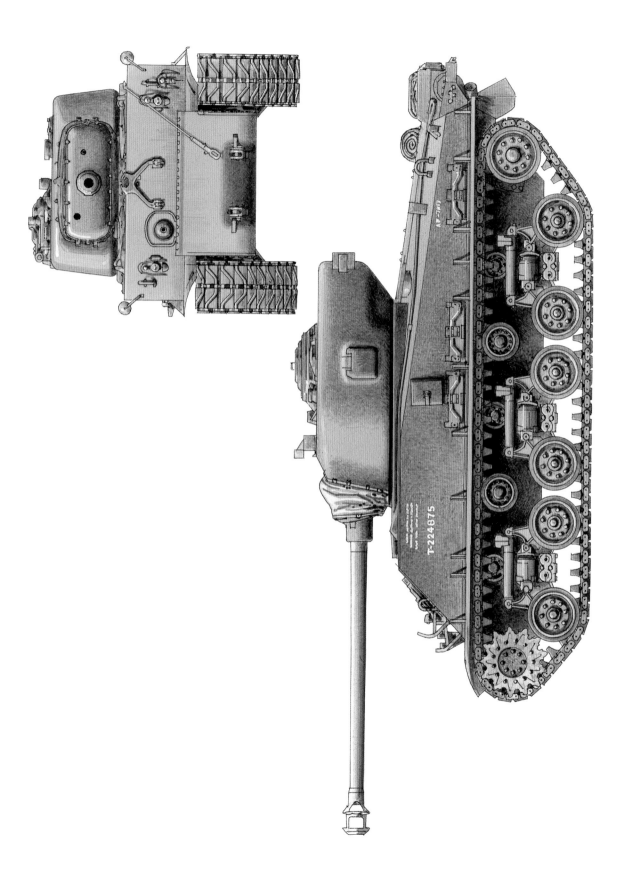

Sherman M4 Firefly with 17-pounder gun

First appearing in January 1944, the Firefly was a British modification of the Sherman that mounted an Ordnance quick-firing (QF) 17-pounder (76.2mm) gun in a heavily modified turret. It was the most powerful Sherman variant of the Second World War. Early development work used the M4 hull (Sherman I – with a 'C' suffix used to indicate the Firefly conversion), as seen here, but many were also based on the M4A4 (Sherman VC); there are suggestions that the M4A1 and M4A3 variants may also have been used.

Note how the gun barrel on this example has been partially camouflaged in an attempt to disguise its length – the major identifying feature of the conversion.

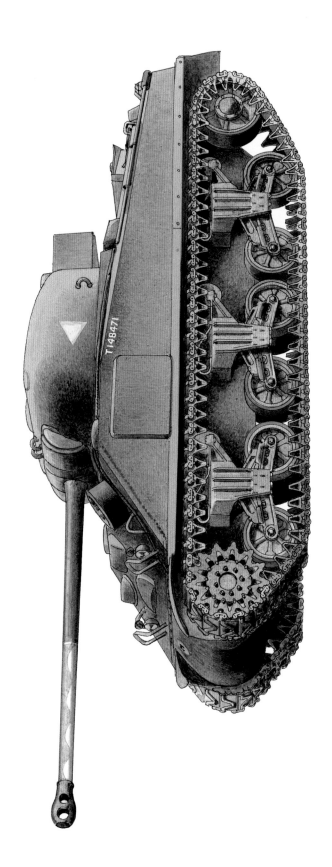

This heavily damaged M4A1 cast-hull Sherman demonstrates the damage that armour-piercing rounds can cause. It had spent some years being used as a hard target on a tank range. (*Warehouse Collection*)

More heavily damaged Sherman hulls, including a rare beach armoured recovery vehicle (BARV). Note the early three-piece cast nose on the hull closest to the camera. (*Warehouse Collection*)

Following the liberation of the city, victory parades were held in Paris on 26 and 29 August 1944, the latter including the US 28th Infantry Division. The photograph shows a Free French welded-hull Sherman followed by an M8 75mm howitzer gun motor carriage based on the chassis of the M5 Stuart light tank. (*Warehouse Collection*)

Although nowhere near as tall as the M3 medium tank, the Sherman nevertheless presented a temptingly prominent silhouette for enemy gunners ... one British tank crewman reflected soberly that 'it was too big' for his liking! (*Ford Motor Company*)

The Germans were more than happy to press into service anything they could capture from the Allies ... the photograph shows a well-marked captured Sherman M4A4 Firefly. Finding suitable ammunition must have been something of a challenge. (*Warehouse Collection*)

Many Shermans remain in Normandy, where they serve as static monuments to the momentous struggle to free Europe. This welded-hull M4A2 overlooks the site of Mulberry B at Arromanches. (*Warehouse Collection*)

Its small size and manoeuvrability made the Sherman ideal for street fighting. This is the Chrysler-engined M4A4. (*US Signal Corps*)

This ex-Israeli Sherman M50 Mk 2, being examined with interest by a US Marine who was probably not born when it was built, was one of a number given to the Christian Militia in Lebanon during the civil war. (*PHC Chet King, US Army*)

A Sherman M4A3E8 – the so-called 'Easy Eight' – photographed during action in Korea in 1951. (*US Signal Corps*)

A knocked-out Egyptian Sherman on the Sinai Peninsula following the 1956 Arab–Israeli conflict. The left-hand track sections appear to have lost the rubber pads. (*Warehouse Collection*)

Chapter Five

The Sherman Described

There is a natural tendency to think of the numerous variants of the Sherman gun tank as a logical progression of development, with the M4 replaced by the improved M4A1, and then by the M4A2, and so on. However, this is not really the case. The different variants were generally developed more in an attempt to counter a shortage of suitable engines, and to allow the tank to be manufactured at multiple locations, rather than to incorporate significant improvements and upgrades. And in most cases the variants were constructed concurrently rather than one replacing another.

That is not to say that the Sherman was not improved during its production life – it just wasn't improved enough. Major upgrades included the substitution of the more powerful 76mm gun for the original 75mm, increases in the levels of armoured protection, and improvements to the suspension, most notably the change to the horizontal volute spring suspension (HVSS) system and wider tracks that represented a distinct advance on the original suspension arrangements. The Anglo-American Firefly, the M4A3E2 'Jumbo' and the up-armoured M4A3E8 (the so-called 'Easy Eight') certainly represent the high point of Sherman development. However, it should be remembered that many of the numerous changes that were made were introduced to simplify the production process and it makes more sense to think of the Sherman gun tank as having been produced with a range of engines, and with the M3 75mm gun, the M1 76mm gun and the M4 105mm howitzer.

The Sherman was of conventional layout for a medium-weight tank of the period, consisting of a low-profile armoured hull, either fabricated from huge castings or made from welded armoured steel plate, with a rotating turret that mounted the main gun together with a co-axial machine gun. The hull was divided into three areas, consisting of the driving compartment at the front, the fighting compartment in the centre, and the engine at the rear; the transmission was at the front of the tank in the driving compartment, and was located between the driver and the co-driver. The turret was placed in the centre of the hull, bolted to the turret ring in such a way that it was free to rotate on a 69in diameter ball race. Entry to and exit from the vehicle were made by means of access hatches, and there was an emergency escape hatch in the floor. Drain valves in the bottom of the hull allowed any accumulated water or fuel to be removed.

Air-recognition features included the cast rounded turret with its right-hand circular hatch, the long wedge-shaped hull and tapering rear deck, with a grille behind the turret, and the way that the hull was extended to cover the tracks. The 76mm gun variant had a large counterweight on the turret rear, and the M4A1 and M4A5 cast-hull variants had a distinctive turtle-shell appearance. Some examples were fitted with sand skirts.

The upper cast hull of the M4A1 and M4A5 consisted of a massive piece of metal, cast in one piece, that sat on top of the welded chassis, into which the automotive components were mounted. Early tanks were fitted with a nose casting that consisted of three separate sections, flange-bolted together, but this was subsequently superseded by a rounded one-piece nose casting that offered improved strength and simplified maintenance; this in turn was superseded by a second type of one-piece casting with a sharper contour and a thicker nose. On the welded-hull tanks, the upper hull was constructed from a number of separate pieces of rolled homogenous armour (RHA), electrically welded together to form a rigid, protective box. The exact number of pieces used depended on the manufacturer's production facilities; for example, the M4A3 hull was constructed from fewer components than the M4A2, which, of course, meant that less welding was required. The so-called M4 'composite' (or hybrid) was constructed with a cast nose and glacis plate that was welded to a fabricated rear section; the cast section extended from the differential housing to the forward edge of the turret ring. This form of construction was also used for the Caterpillar-engined M4A6.

All of the hulls had welded lifting eyes at the front and rear corners, to allow the upper and lower hulls to be separated, or to lift the tank for loading, and towing shackles were welded to the lower nose casting. A travelling lock, in the form of a large clamp that secured the gun barrel, was welded to the glacis plate on later production examples.

In an attempt to improve the ballistic performance of the Sherman hull, rectangular *appliqué* armour plates, 1 in thick, were welded to the outside of the hull adjacent to the ammunition storage bins and the fuel tanks. *Appliqué* patches were also welded to the glacis plate immediately in front of the driver's and co-driver's positions, and additional armour was applied to the right-hand front face of the turret where the casting had been reduced in thickness to accommodate the powered traverse gear. Those tanks armed with the 105mm howitzer had additional internal armour protecting the ammunition racks.

The engine was mounted in the rear of the hull, with access into the engine compartment available via side-hinged doors. Six different types of engine were used, with the changes to the basic designation identifying which was which; variations were made to the hull to accommodate the different engines. In all cases the engine rotated anti-clockwise when viewed from the nose, and a long, two-part propeller shaft conveyed power beneath the floor to the transmission and final drive assembly, which was mounted in the front of the hull.

The M4, the M4A1 and the M4A5 were fitted with a nine-cylinder air-cooled overhead-valve supercharged radial engine of 15,928cc (972in^3), originally running on minimum 92-octane petrol but subsequently redesigned for 80-octane fuel. These engines, which were manufactured by either Wright or Continental, were originally designated as the 'Ordnance Engine R-975-EC2'; the first modification was the R-975-C1, with a maximum power output of 400bhp at 4,000rpm; this was subsequently superseded by the R-975-C4, where the power output was increased to 460bhp.

The M4A2 was powered by a twin diesel engine set-up manufactured by the Detroit Diesel Division of General Motors and designated as the 6046D. Consisting of two GM 6-71 six-cylinder water-cooled overhead-valve, overhead-cam two-stroke supercharged diesel engines installed side-by-side, the maximum power output from a combined capacity of 13,929cc (850in^3) was stated as 410bhp at 2,900rpm, and the engines were designed to run on 40-cetane diesel fuel. There was no conventional fuel-injector pump, and the injectors were cycled directly by the camshafts. For starting the engines in extreme cold weather, a hand pump could be used to inject Kigass (ether) into the inlet manifolds, with a small trembler coil provided for a form of conventional ignition.

Power for the M4A3 was provided by the Ford GAA-III engine, a normally aspirated water-cooled V8 overhead valve unit with a capacity of 18,026cc (1,100in^3), which had been designed expressly for use in tanks. The maximum power output, running on 80-octane petrol, was 500bhp at 2,600rpm. This was the engine favoured by the US Army.

Chrysler's curious thirty-cylinder side-valve multi-bank A-57 petrol engine was fitted to the M4A4, consisting, effectively, of five separate water-cooled six-cylinder petrol engines arranged in a star configuration around a common crankcase. The maximum power output was stated as 425bhp at 2,850rpm from a combined capacity of 20,533cc (1,253in^3).

Finally the M4A6, which never entered volume production, was powered by a Caterpillar nine-cylinder air-cooled supercharged radial diesel engine with overhead valves, designed to produce 497bhp at 3,000rpm from a capacity of 29,847cc (1,823in^3) when running on 40-cetane diesel fuel. Designated D-200A by its makers, and identified as the 'Ordnance engine RD-1820', this was an early example of a military multi-fuel engine and it was equally capable of running on high- or low-octane petrol, crude oil, etc.

The Ford GAA-III engine was installed lower in the hull than the radial engines, which allowed a lower floor, giving greater clearance under the turret basket. On the other hand, the height of the Caterpillar RD-1820 engine necessitated the use of an additional drop-gear transfer case, which brought the output of the engine down to the standard prop-shaft position and allowed the propeller shaft speed to be increased by 50 per cent when compared to the crankshaft speed. Regardless of type, the engine faced to the rear, with the radiators for the water-cooled Ford, Detroit Diesel and Chrysler units placed up against the rear wall of the hull, with cooling air drawn through the grilled engine deck. The air-cooled engines were fitted with a large fan on the crankshaft nose, drawing cooling air through ducts and across the cylinders. With both the GM twin diesel engines and the Chrysler A-57 multi-bank, space in the engine compartment was at something of a premium, which did not simplify maintenance. The engines drew fuel from four tanks, two located in the rear sponson and two in the front corners of the engine compartment, the total fuel capacity depending on the specific variant. Fuel fillers were placed on the rear deck, between the rear of the turret and the air intake grilles.

All Sherman variants were also fitted with a single-cylinder Homelite HRUH-28 air-cooled two-stroke auxiliary engine of 154cc. This engine was coupled to a 30V 50Ah generator designed to charge the batteries while the main engine was shut down, and to supplement the charge rate of the generator driven by the main engine.

Drive was transmitted to the gearbox and final drive system through a Borg & Beck or Lipe double-disc dry clutch assembly. The transmission was bolted into the nose of the tank, and consisted of a five-speed manual gearbox with a single reverse gear, protected by a push-button interlock, together with a controlled differential that incorporated the steering brakes. An oil cooler was installed in conjunction with the differential to maintain the transmission oil at an appropriate temperature.

The flame-cut drive sprockets, which were located at the front of the tank, were coupled to the differential shafts through a set of reduction gears and were bolted directly to the final drive shafts. At the rear the idler wheels were spoked on early production vehicles and solid on later versions. All of the US-built machines used a thirteen-tooth sprocket and the track pitch was 6in; on the Canadian M4A5 an additional tooth was required to suit the shorter pitch (4.6in) track shoes. Each track run consisted of seventy-nine shoes (eighty-three for the extended hull M4A4 and M4A6), supported on the top run by three return rollers. A number of designs of both steel and rubber-faced track shoe were used, not least because rubber tracks were expensive in terms of the materials consumed, at a time when the Japanese were controlling something like 90 per cent of the world's supply of natural rubber. One set of rubber tracks, together with spare shoes, consumed around 1,734lb of

Cast-hull M4A1E8 with HVSS suspension at the Pennsylvania Military Museum in Boalsburgh, Pennsylvania. Developed by the Chrysler Corporation and adopted as standard for all medium tanks from August 1944, the HVSS suspension allowed the use of wider tracks with paired bogie wheels, and gave a much improved ride. (*Les Duplock*)

An early Ford-built M4A3 showing the clean lines of the welded hull. The VVSS suspension on this tank has the trailing support roller with a spring steel track skid on top of the bogie mounting. (*Ford Motor Company*)

rubber. The change to steel tracks was made in late 1942, and from 1944 steel tracks were being manufactured with a rubber coating.

Two types of steering system were employed during the life of the vehicle, although both operated directly onto the differential output shafts via a system of rods and levers. Described as either 'single-' or 'double-anchor brakes', each consisted of a band of three brake shoes acting on the external face of the brake drums and contained in an oil bath. The brakes were applied via a pair of levers, spring-loaded to a forward position. Pulling back on one lever applied the brakes to that particular track, causing the differential to apply more power to the un-braked track; pulling back equally on both levers would bring the tank to a halt in a straight line. The design of the differential did not allow the tank to execute a neutral turn, where the tracks rotate in opposite directions, and even applying the brake to one track to cause a full skid turn called for considerable effort. Both brakes could be latched in the on position when the tank was parked.

The suspension and track-return components were attached directly to the lower part of the hull and consisted of three bogie assemblies on either side, with the rubber-tyred road wheels attached to leading and trailing arms between which was a large, vertical volute spring. Three support rollers were provided for the upper run of the tracks. On early production vehicles the support rollers were mounted directly on the top of the suspension units, but later production saw them moved to the rear of the suspension unit, with a spring-steel skid on top; three different designs of skid were used before the VVSS suspension was replaced. The longer hull of the M4A4 (and M4A6) placed the suspension units further apart than on the other variants, with the bogie centres increased from 57in to 63.675in.

In early 1942 the original VVSS suspension had been superseded by an upgraded heavy-duty version in which the original 7in diameter springs were replaced by 8in springs, but the later M4A3E8 variant – the 'Easy Eight' – and the M4A3E9 were both fitted with the much-improved horizontal volute spring suspension (HVSS) system that had been developed by the Chrysler Corporation. This allowed the use of wider tracks with paired bogie wheels, and gave a much improved ride. The HVSS suspension became standard for all medium tanks from August 1944. In the British Army system of identification for the Sherman, tanks that were fitted with the HVSS system were given a 'Y' suffix, e.g., 'Sherman IIIAY'.

Three basic turret designs were used; the first was intended for the 75mm and 105mm guns, the second for the later 76mm weapon, and the third was used only for the M4A3E2 assault tank. All three were of cast construction. The original turret was almost circular in plan and had a sloping front, a gently rounded profile and a flat roof. A pistol port was fitted into the left-hand side wall, only to be eliminated ... and subsequently reinstated over a period of months. A turret basket provided a mounting for the commander's, gunner's and loader's seats and a floor to the fighting compartment. The turret roof incorporated a rotating commander's cupola with six 3in prismatic vision blocks giving a wide field of view, an access hatch for the loader (from 1943 on), and a powered exhaust fan(s) to keep the interior clear of gun fumes during firing. The second turret, designed for the M1 76mm gun, was altogether squarer in shape, and had a large counterweight at the rear. The turret basket was modified, and later eliminated altogether, which meant that the seats for the commander and the loader had to be carried on the turret rim. The third style of turret resembled that used for the 76mm gun, but the sides were of considerably heavier construction.

With a diameter of 69in, the turret ring was felt to be the largest that could be accommodated on the hull without compromising strength, and the turret itself, regardless of type, was carried on a ball race that allowed a full 360 degrees traverse. The bearing race was recessed to prevent the entry of bullet splash and to protect the race from direct hits. Both the 75mm and 76mm gun tanks were fitted with hydraulic powered traverse systems supplied by the Oilgear Company; a lack of sufficient production at Oilgear meant that some tanks were fitted either with a hydraulic traverse system produced by Logansport, or with an electric traverse system from the Westinghouse Company, neither of which apparently offered the smoothness of operation of the Oilgear equipment. Tanks equipped with the 105mm howitzer did not have power-traversing gear for the turret.

As regards the main gun, four different weapons were used, with calibres of 75mm, 76mm and 105mm; there was also the British 17-pounder (76.2mm) that was retro-fitted into the Firefly.

The 75mm gun was produced in two versions but only the first two Shermans to be constructed were fitted with the original short-barrelled M2 weapon, which had a length-to-calibre ratio of L/32. This gun is easily identified by the two large counterweights clamped around the muzzle. The second of the two tanks fitted with this weapon was subsequently converted to the standard M3 75mm configuration.

The M2 75mm gun was almost immediately replaced by the longer-barrelled M3 75mm gun, carried in either the M34 or M34A1 mount, which allowed a maximum elevation of +25 degrees, and a maximum depression of −12 degrees (−10 degrees for the later M34A1 mount). The M34A1 mount, fitted from October 1942, had a larger rotor shield and a direct-sighting telescope. It weighed some 893lb, and the overall length of the gun was 118.38in, giving a length-to-calibre ratio of L/40.1; the bore was machined with twenty-four grooves, with a uniform right-hand twist at a rate of one turn in 25.59 calibres. The breech was the semi-automatic sliding wedge type, with the gun mounted so that the breech slid into place vertically from the right-hand side. The maximum rate of fire was twenty rounds a minute, and the muzzle velocity was 2,030ft/sec using armour-piercing capped (APC) ammunition, giving a theoretical armour-piercing capability of about 48mm at 2,000yd.

Authorised ammunition types for the M3 gun, all of them of the 'fixed' or one-piece configuration, included armour-piercing solid shot (AP); armour-piercing solid shot with tracer (AP-T); armour-piercing capped (APC); armour-piercing capped with tracer (APC-T); armour-piercing capped, ballistic capped (APCBC); hyper-velocity armour-piercing (HVAP); hyper-velocity armour-piercing with tracer (HVAP-T); hyper-velocity target practice with tracer (HVTP-T); high explosive (HE), either with impact, 'superquick' or variable delay fuse; high explosive with tracer (HEP-T); and white phosphorous smoke (WP, or 'Willy Peter') rounds. Blank and drill practice rounds were also available.

From August 1942 there had been experiments with M4A1 Shermans fitted with the 3in M7 gun of the M10 tank destroyer, but there was insufficient space in the turret to allow proper operation, and the installation was never felt to be satisfactory. In July 1943 two experimental M4E6 variants were fitted with what was described as the M1 76mm gun carried in mount M62, giving a maximum elevation of +25 degrees, and a maximum depression −12 degrees. A new cast turret was designed to suit the gun and mount. Although subsequent events proved that the new gun was scarcely an improvement on what had gone before, the M1 was designed to fire the same projectiles as the M7 gun of the M10, and the M4E6 was approved for production a month later. The new gun weighed 1,141lb, and had an overall length of 163.75in, giving a length-to-calibre figure of L/54.6; the original gun was soon replaced in production by the M1A1 variant in which the barrel length was reduced to give a length-to-calibre ratio of L/52 and at the same time a small counterweight was added to the muzzle. The bore was machined with twenty-eight grooves, having a uniform right-hand twist at a rate of one turn in forty calibres; the M1A2 variant had the pitch of the rifling reduced to thirty-two calibres and provision was made for fitting a muzzle brake. Like the M3 75mm, the breech was a semi-automatic sliding wedge, but the gun was mounted so that the breech slid into place horizontally. The maximum rate of fire was also twenty rounds a minute, but the muzzle velocity was increased to 2,600ft/sec using armour-piercing capped (APC) ammunition, giving a theoretical armour-piercing capability of 75mm at 2,000yd, with a maximum range of 16,100yd.

Authorised standard ammunition types for the M1 76mm gun included armour-piercing solid shot (AP); armour-piercing solid shot with tracer (AP-T); armour-piercing capped (APC); armour-piercing capped with tracer (APC-T); hyper-velocity armour-piercing (HVAP); hyper-velocity armour-piercing with tracer (HVAP-T); hyper-velocity target practice with tracer (HVTP-T); high explosive (HE), either with impact, 'superquick' or variable delay fuse; high explosive with tracer (HEP-T); and white phosphorous smoke (WP) rounds. Again, there were also blank and drill practice rounds.

The third standard Sherman gun was the M4 105mm howitzer, effectively a modified version of the gun used in the American M2A1 towed howitzer; in fact, the M2A1 variant of the gun had been used in trials, but was deemed unsatisfactory because of difficulties experienced in loading in the confined space of the Sherman turret. Carried in the T70 or M52 mount, which provided a maximum elevation of +35 degrees, and a maximum depression of −10 degrees, the gun still had to be mounted on its side, meaning that the manually operated sliding-wedge breech was loaded horizontally rather than from the top. The bore was machined with thirty-six grooves, having a uniform right-hand twist at a rate of one turn in twenty calibres, and the overall length was 101.3in, giving a length-to-calibre ratio of L/24.5. The maximum rate of fire was eight rounds a minute, and the muzzle velocity was 1,550ft/sec using high-explosive (HE) ammunition, allowing the weapon to penetrate 102mm of armour at any effective range.

In common with most artillery weapons of the period, a separate bagged charge was used in the howitzer, allowing the appropriate charge to be selected to best suit the mission. Authorised standard ammunition types included high-explosive (HE); high-explosive anti-tank (HEAT); impact-fused high-explosive (HE); and various types of smoke and chemical rounds.

The Sherman Firefly was equipped with the British Ordnance quick-firing (QF) 17-pounder (76.2mm) gun in either Mk IV or Mk VII form. As with the American 105mm howitzer, the sheer size of the gun meant that it had to be turned onto its side to fit into the turret; a large hole was cut in the rear wall of the turret to accommodate the recoil, and was protected by an armoured box. The gun was carried in the British 'mounting, number 2, Mk I', which provided a maximum elevation of +20 degrees, and a maximum depression of −5 degrees. The overall length of the gun was 184.1in, giving a length-to-calibre ratio of L/58.3, and the bore was machined with twenty grooves having a uniform right-hand twist at a rate of one turn in thirty calibres. The maximum rate of fire was ten rounds a minute, and the muzzle velocity was 3,950ft/sec using armour-piercing discarding sabot tracer (APDS-T) ammunition; theoretical armour-piercing capability was 161mm at a range of 2,000yd.

Suitable ammunition types for the 17-pounder (76.2mm) gun included armour-piercing capped, ballistic capped (APCBC); armour-piercing discarding sabot (APDS); armour-piercing discarding sabot with tracer (APDS-T); and impact-fused high explosive (HE) rounds.

Both the 75mm and 76mm Sherman gun tanks were fitted with a single-plane hydraulic gyro-stabiliser that, in theory, allowed the gun to be fired with a reasonable degree of accuracy while the tank was on the move. The equipment maintained the main gun, and the co-axial machine gun, at a predetermined elevation from the vertical, subject to small manual corrections from the gunner.

Constant changes were made to the detailed specification of the vision equipment during the Sherman's production life, but in principle each crew member was provided with indirect vision equipment using either periscopes or, on early production models, direct-vision slots protected by hinged covers; the latter were very susceptible to bullet splash. The gunner's periscope was synchronised with the gun and contained a telescopic sight with a ballistic reticule; the later designs for the gunner's periscope incorporated two telescopes, one for close targets and the other for long-range work. Towards the end of the production run an azimuth indicator was installed to assist with accuracy of indirect fire.

Ammunition for the main gun was stowed inside the hull, originally in open racks in the side sponsons, as well as beneath the gun itself and behind the co-driver's seat. The number of rounds carried was 97 for tanks with a welded hull (104 in the M4A3E2), and 90 in the cast hulls. Additional stowage was provided below the floor on tanks equipped with the 76mm gun, and this necessitated cutting away most of the floor of the turret basket, as a bonus making considerably more space in the fighting compartment. It soon became apparent that the ammunition was vulnerable to catching fire if enemy hits penetrated the upper areas of the hull, and a short-term solution to this problem involved welding *appliqué* armour patches to the outer face of the hull side plates. A more satisfactory solution was the adoption of so-called 'wet' ammunition storage in 1944, where the ammunition was placed in water-protected racks below the turret ... this change is said to have affected 2,500 separate items and required considerable detailed redesigning of the interior. Sherman designations that include a 'W' suffix (e.g. M4A3W) indicate that the tank in question had wet ammunition stowage facilities.

A towing pintle provided at the rear of the hull was designed to allow the Sherman to tow the rubber-tyred M8 ammunition trailer. The trailer was designed to carry ninety-three rounds for either the 75mm or 76mm gun, or forty-two rounds for the 105mm howitzer.

Secondary weapons included two M1919A4 0.30in machine guns, one mounted co-axially to the left of the main gun, the other in a ball mount in the nose of the tank designed to be operated by the co-driver. A Browning M2 0.50in machine gun was generally carried in an anti-aircraft mount on the forward part of the commander's cupola, although for a short period between September 1942 and April 1943 this was replaced by a 0.30in weapon. There was also a 2in M3 mortar mounted on the turret roof to lay down a smokescreen. Very early production vehicles had two additional 0.30in machine guns on a tandem mount in the forward part of the hull.

There was also space inside the hull for stowing between 4,000 and 6,250 rounds for the machine guns, the exact number depending on the variant, and between twelve and twenty-seven 2in smoke bombs. A tripod was carried that would allow either of the 0.30in machine guns to be dismounted and fired from the ground.

All of the Sherman variants were wired on a 24V electrical system, using two large 12V batteries located in the left sponson that were coupled in series to supply power for the engine electrical systems, the interior lighting, the gun-control equipment, the turret traverse system (where electrically operated), the windscreen wiper and the external lighting. Late model tanks incorporated a heating coil to protect the batteries from extreme cold. A master switch allowed the batteries to be isolated, and a 12V sub-circuit was provided for the radio and other communications equipment. Automatic breakers were provided to protect the various circuits, and all of the wiring was carried in metal conduits, both to protect the cables and to provide a measure of radio suppression. Power was transferred to the turret via seven copper collector rings, each with its own contact brush.

A box-shaped instrument panel was located in the left-hand sponson adjacent to the driving position. The panel included a speedometer, rev counter (tachometer), ammeter, gauges to show the engine oil-pressure, fuel level and water temperature, and warning lights for low oil pressure and excessive water temperature; on twin-engined vehicles certain of the gauges were duplicated. There were also switches for the lighting equipment, the fuel cut-off valves and the vehicle starter, as well as a selector switch for the four fuel tanks. A row of push-button thermal circuit breakers were provided to protect the various circuits.

Radio equipment, consisting of an FM or AM radio set, was installed in the turret bustle. In the US Army standard FM (frequency modulation) sets included the Signals Corps SCR-508, SCR-528, SCR-538 or SCR-608B, each of which had a range of somewhere between 5 and 20 miles depending on local conditions, or the AM (amplitude modulation) set AN/VRC-3. The infantry telephone extension was designated RC-298. A command tank might also have been equipped with an SCR-506, SCR-245 or SCR-193 in the right-hand sponson. In the British and Canadian Armies the standard radio was either the Number 19 or Number 29 set, both offering a range of up to 25 miles.

View of the transmission and the driver's position on the cut-away Sherman at the Canadian Museum of War, Ottawa. (*Bachcell*)

(*Opposite top*) Sectional view of the Chrysler-powered M4A4; note the increased spacing of the bogies to accommodate the lengthened hull. (*Chrysler Corporation*)

(*Opposite below*) In the hybrid cast/welded hull of the M4 'composite' the upper front part of the hull was formed from a single casting, welded to the remainder of the hull ahead of the turret ring. These tanks were constructed only at the Detroit Tank Arsenal. (*David Doyle*)

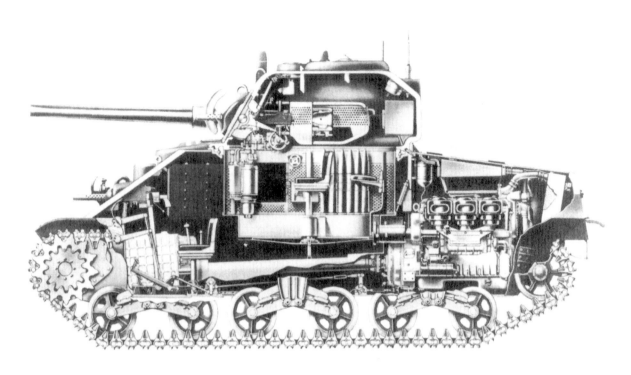

The nose of the hull, which supported the differential and final-drive assembly, originally consisted of three separate castings bolted together via flanges. (*Warehouse Collection*)

This M4A3 demonstrates the modifications made to the hull when the original three-piece cast differential housing was replaced by a one-piece casting that made it easier to assemble the transmission, as well as providing additional stiffness. (*Ford Motor Company*)

Designed by the Wright Aeronautical Division of the Curtiss-Wright Corporation, and also produced under licence by the Continental Aircraft Engine Company, the R-975 was a nine-cylinder, supercharged radial petrol engine producing 340–460bhp from 15,928cc, according to the stage of development. This engine was used in the M4, M4A1 and M4A5 variants. (*Warehouse Collection*)

(*Opposite top*) The twin-engine 6046D power unit of the M4A2 consisted of a pair of GM 6-71 supercharged two-stroke diesel truck engines installed side-by-side with the power collected together via a transfer box. The power output was 410bhp from a combined capacity of 13,929cc. (*General Motors Corporation*)

(*Opposite below*) Ford's mighty GAA-III V8 petrol engine produced 500bhp from its 18,026cc capacity and was almost certainly the best engine fitted to the Sherman. Production of the engine continued even after Ford was no longer involved in building Shermans. (*Ford Motor Company*)

Consisting of five six-cylinder petrol engines assembled, star fashion, around a common crankcase, the Chrysler A-57 engine of the M4A4 was unnecessarily complex, but had the advantage of not requiring too much development. Power output was 425bhp from a combined capacity of 20,533cc. (*Chrysler Corporation*)

(*Opposite top*) All Shermans were equipped with a 154cc single-cylinder Homelite HRUH-28 air-cooled two-stroke auxiliary engine, coupled to a 30V 50Ah generator designed to charge the batteries while the main engine was shut down. The photograph shows this engine in its early configuration. (*Ford Motor Company*)

(*Opposite below*) The gearbox and final-drive assembly viewed from the drive end; the transmission casting also forms the lower glacis plate of the hull. (*Warehouse Collection*)

Until August 1944 all Shermans were equipped with the vertical volute spring suspension (VVSS) system. There were four variants of the system; the track support roller was originally carried on top of the bogie mounting, and, once the roller was moved to the trailing arm shown here, there were three different patterns of track skid. (*Warehouse Collection*)

The horizontal volute spring suspension (HVSS) system, fitted to all Sherman variants with the 'E8' suffix, employed paired parallel bogie wheels, together with a different arrangement of springs. This allowed the use of wider tracks that also contributed to the improved ride. (*Warehouse Collection*)

A 75mm gun barrel being fitted into the early M34 mount. (*Ford Motor Company*)

Interior view of the hull showing some of the stowage arrangements. The unprotected 75mm rounds contributed to the frequency with which a Sherman that had been hit and penetrated would brew-up. The later wet ammunition stowage arrangements were a considerable improvement in this respect. (*Ford Motor Company*)

A British Number 19 radio set installed in the turret bustle. (*Ford Motor Company*)

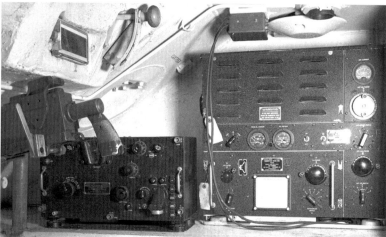

A US Army radio BC312-D high-frequency radio receiver and TU-6-B transmitter tuning unit installed in the right-hand sponson. Together these pieces of equipment formed part of radio set SCR-193 as installed in a command tank. (*Ford Motor Company*)

An experimental all-round vision cupola was developed by Dr Pochin of the Medical Research Council. Designed to be fitted to the Sherman turret by means of a special ring, the cupola incorporated eight periscopes, and was interchangeable with similar cupolas fitted to Churchill and Cromwell tanks. It was not adopted for service. (*Warehouse Collection*)

Chapter Six

Improving the Breed

While the M4A6 might have been the final official iteration of the M4, at least in numerical terms, the numbers of Shermans in use around the world were such that development didn't halt when the last example was constructed. Even though the construction of new tanks ceased in 1945, the Sherman remained big business, with money to be made from selling upgrades, and a number of nations operating Shermans put the tanks through an improvement programme using either their own or third-party equipment.

During the Second World War the most notable Sherman gun tank adaptation was the Anglo-American Sherman Firefly – or Mayfly, as it was sometimes called at the time. Based on existing M4 'composite' M4A1, M4A3, M4A4 and M4A5 tanks, the Firefly mounted a modified turret into which was placed the British 17-pounder (76.2mm) Ordnance quick-firing (OQF) gun. The modification had started life as a similarly equipped development of the British A27M Cromwell tank, mounting the 17-pounder (76.2mm) gun in a new cast turret that had been produced by Stothert & Pitt. Designated the A30 Challenger, the finished product was heavily criticised, even to the extent of being described as a 'white elephant'. One of its most severe critics, Lieutenant Colonel George Witheridge, believed that there was nothing wrong with the 17-pounder (76.2mm) gun ... but that it would be better fitted into the Sherman, a feat that one Major George Brighty managed to pull off using the standard turret!

Despite many still believing that the project was not really feasible, the Sherman Firefly was supported by Sir Claude Gibb, Director General of Weapon and Instrument Production at the Ministry of Supply (MoS), and was sponsored by General Raymond Briggs. It was clear that considerable modification would be required to the turret, and the early conversion work that led to the vehicle being approved for production was carried out by Vickers-Armstrong. Despite the breech block effectively having to lie on its side in order to provide sufficient space to load the gun, successful firing trials were carried out in February 1944, and production started later in the year, with the Royal Ordnance Factory, Leeds contracted to convert around 2,100–2,350 examples. The Firefly conversion was identified by adding a 'C' suffix to the basic British designation (e.g., Sherman VC).

There is no doubt that the Firefly was enormously successful, with some authorities stating that it was the best tank available to the Allies during the Second World War ... even some American commanders demanded that they be equipped with one Firefly in each medium tank platoon deployed in north-west Europe. Although the new gun did nothing to counter the relative weakness of the Sherman hull when compared to the heavier German tanks, it did at least provide the Allies with a tank that had sufficient hitting power to confront the Germans on a more equal footing.

Many other development vehicles were also produced during the Second World War with a view to eventually allowing possible upgrades to the production vehicles. Few were actually put into production, and most were abandoned. See Table 2, page 138.

During the 1950s the emerging nation state of Israel was an enthusiastic user of Shermans; as the vehicles started to show their age, the Israeli Defence Force (IDF) devised a programme of upgrades, both to the engine and to the main gun, reputedly devoting as much as 2,500 man-hours to each tank. The chosen gun was a modified version of the French CN-75-50, a high-velocity 75mm weapon produced by Giat that was based on the *KwK.42 L/70* of the German *Panther* tank. The same Giat gun was also used in the IDF AMX-13 tanks, so there was a useful degree of commonality. Work started in 1953/54, and the converted turrets and guns were supplied direct from France, with the conversion work carried out in IDF workshops. The IDF initially used M4A4 hulls in which the Chrysler multi-bank engine had been replaced by the Wright or Continental R-975 radial, but after some fifty or so vehicles had been converted a switch was made to later M4A3 hulls fitted with the horizontal volute spring suspension (HVSS). At the same time the radial engines were replaced by a Cummins VT-8-460Bi V8 turbocharged diesel engine producing 460bhp, which was coupled to the original transmission. Often described as the 'Super Sherman', the resulting vehicle was officially designated Sherman M50.

A decade or so later a further 180 IDF M4A1 HVSS Shermans were up-gunned, this time using a shortened version of the more-powerful 105mm French Giat CN-105F1 low-pressure gun, which was built under licence in Israel. Also powered by a Cummins VT-8-460Bi diesel engine, these tanks can be recognised by the huge turret bustle that was required to counterbalance the weight of the gun. Designated Sherman M51 (and sometimes unofficially described as the 'Isherman'), the first example was shown in public in May 1965. The M51 saw action in both the 1967 and 1973 Arab–Israeli conflicts and a number remained in service into the 1980s, when they were replaced by the home-grown Merkava main battle tank.

However, this was not yet the end of the road for the Sherman. As late as 1980/81 the prestigious defence industry directory *Janes Armour and Artillery* was still reporting that Shermans – including some Fireflys – remained in service with Argentina, Chile, Colombia, Ecuador, Israel, Nicaragua, Pakistan, Paraguay, Peru, South

Africa and Yugoslavia. Sherman-based armoured recovery vehicles (ARV) were also still in widespread use. Even at this late date, with the youngest of the tanks approaching their quarter of a century, the sheer numbers of Shermans available, combined with factors such as ease of operation and basic reliability, meant that the vehicle was still an ideal candidate for upgrade. To counter the difficulties with the original engine, Argentina had chosen to fit their Shermans with the French-built Poyaud 520 V8 S2 diesel engine, while the Israeli company NIMDA offered retrofit power-packs tailored specifically for each Sherman variant, using the GM Detroit Diesel 8V-71T diesel engine in conjunction with the original front-mounted transmission. And it is worth recording that the last Sherman to serve with the Cuban Revolutionary Armed Forces was rebuilt in 1981 with a V12 multi-fuel diesel engine taken from a Soviet T-54 or T-55 main battle tank to allow it to participate in a movie about the revolution ... oh, the shame of it!

Even as late as 1990 the US company NAPCO Industries and Israeli Military Industries were both still offering diesel power-pack upgrades for the Sherman. The latter were also claiming to have supplied 'a quantity' of Shermans to an undisclosed end user in 1987 that had been upgraded with a new diesel power-pack, as well as the company's 60mm hyper-velocity medium support weapon (HVMS-60) and a new fire-control system.

The IDF also used obsolete Shermans as the basis for a range of heavily modified specialised engineers' vehicles, including this medevac vehicle constructed on the lower hull and running gear of an M4A3E8. (*Bukvoed*)

The Sherman Firefly was fitted with the British 17-pounder (76.2mm) Ordnance quick-firing (OQF) gun. This was the only Sherman variant able to tackle the heavier German tanks on a more-or-less equal basis. This M4A1 Firefly saw post-war service in South Africa. (*Warehouse Collection*)

A Sherman Firefly photographed on the streets of Hamburg in the spring of 1945. (*US Signal Corps*)

The Israeli Defence Force (IDF) M50 'Super Sherman' was equipped with a modified version of the French 75mm CN-75-50 high-velocity gun. The gun, which was developed by Giat, was based on the *KwK.42 L/70* of the German *Panther* tank. (*Bukvoed*)

The 75mm CN-75-50 gun of the M50 Super Sherman necessitated the addition of a large counterweight on the rear of the turret. (*Warehouse Collection*)

Chapter Seven

Sherman Engineers' Tanks

The origins of what are generally called 'engineers' tanks' date back to the earliest days of tank warfare, when in 1917 the British Army modified a number of their Mk IV heavy tanks to facilitate the crossing of deep ditches or trenches. The tanks were adapted to carry fascine bundles or hollow timber cylinders that could be dropped into the ditch in such a way that the tank could drive across it. Mk IV and Mk V tanks were also equipped as bridging tanks by being fitted with hinged ramps to provide a means of crossing other obstacles. Others had their armaments removed and were adapted for use as supply vehicles or gun carriers, while the armoured recovery vehicle was developed by the simple expedient of attaching a jib and pulley block, or a powered crane, to the front of an older or obsolete tank. After the Armistice was signed in 1918 development of the machines generally came to a halt, with few special tanks produced during the interwar years. The outbreak of the Second World War brought a resurgence of interest in using what were essentially modified tanks for specialised roles, particularly for recovering disabled armoured vehicles, a task that was often beyond the capabilities of existing wheeled heavy tractors.

Engineers' tanks really came into their own during the D-Day landings. In the months preceding the invasion a range of so-called 'funnies' was developed, each tasked with overcoming a particular problem, and these vehicles made an enormous contribution to the success of the landings. The fact that the Sherman was plentiful, simple in construction and above all reliable made it the ideal choice for producing a whole range of these specialised vehicles, for example flail tanks, mine-clearing devices, rocket-launchers and flame-throwers. Most of the conversions were 'official', but others, including the mounting of a double-track assault bridge on the Sherman nose, were field modifications made in response to the changing situation on the ground ... and the US authorities did not necessarily always agree with what the British were doing to 'their' tanks.

The US Army's M32 tank recovery vehicle was the only Sherman engineer tank variant to be produced in significant volume, and the pilot model, built by Lima Locomotive in 1943, was constructed on the hull of a standard M4 from which the gun and turret had been removed. It was originally designated TRV (tank recovery vehicle) T5, and changes from the standard gun tank specification included the addition of a large, fixed superstructure mounted in place of the turret, and an 81mm smoke-laying mortar fitted to the top of the hull. A 60,000lb winch was installed in the fighting compartment, and there was a pivoting A-frame jib on the hull, mounted in such a way that it could be used in conjunction with the winch. Additional tow points and equipment stowage facilities were also provided. The design was standardised as the M32 in September 1943. Later variants included the M32B1, based on the hull of the M4A1; the M32B2, which used the M4A2 hull; the M32B3, using the hull of the M4A3, including some examples with HVSS suspension; and the M32B4, which used the M4A4 hull, but never made it into production. As well as Lima Locomotive, M32 recovery vehicles were constructed by the Baldwin Locomotive Works, Federal Machine & Welder, International Harvester and Pressed Steel Car.

Entering service in 1944, the M32B1 was also converted into a prime mover for heavy artillery by the removal of the A-frame; in this form it was designated 'full track prime mover M34'.

The British Army also used the M32 recovery vehicle, describing it as the 'armoured recovery vehicle (ARV) Mk III', but the workshops of the Royal Electrical and Mechanical Engineers (REME) also constructed a 'British' Sherman-based recovery vehicle that they designated 'ARV Mk II'. The vehicle incorporated three winches – a Croft 60-ton winch installed in the fighting compartment, a detachable 3.5-ton winch at the front, and a fixed 9.5-ton winch at the rear; there was also a substantial earth anchor designed to hold the vehicle in place during heavy 'pulls'. In order to camouflage the significance of the vehicle, there was also a fixed 'turret' in which was installed a dummy gun.

REME also developed a more specialised vehicle for recovering drowned or disabled tanks, or other vehicles, from the D-Day landing beaches. Based on the hull of a Sherman from which the turret and gun had been removed, the so-called beach armoured recovery vehicle (BARV) had the hull sides extended in height by the addition of face-hardened armoured plate. Although the driver was reliant on instructions from the commander, the vehicle was able to wade in up to 8ft of water without being swamped. A wooden pusher pad on the nose minimised the possibility of damage when soft-skinned vehicles were being recovered.

Equally well known for their role on the D-Day beaches are the so-called 'duplex-drive' (DD) amphibious tanks. Surprisingly, the British Army had actually started to test amphibious tanks during the First World War, but development did not reach a stage where the vehicles were considered to be reliable. It wasn't until June 1941 that the Hungarian inventor Nicholas Straussler finally solved the problem of making tanks float by the simple expedient of fitting a folding heavy canvas screen to a frame welded around the top of the hull. With the tank in the water, this increased the displacement of the hull to the point where the tank was able to float with the hull below the waterline. Compressed air was used to raise the screen, and it was held in place by mechanical stays. A second drive system transferred power from the track drive sprockets to rear-mounted propellers, and steering was achieved by means of a rudder, and by rotating the propeller mountings in a horizontal plane.

Much impressed by Straussler's folding screen, Major General Percy Hobart of the British 79th Armoured Division carried out swimming trials in Portsmouth harbour, and the success of these trials led to the selection of the British Valentine for the development of the duplex-drive tank. At the same time plans were also put in hand to convert Shermans for the role. Although most of the American, British and Canadian DD tank crews did their preliminary training using Valentines, it quickly became apparent that the Sherman was more suitable for amphibious use and both M4A2 and M4A4 variants were modified. The drive to the propellers was taken from the rear sprockets using bevel gears, which meant that the tracks were running as soon as the tank touched the beach, and the propellers were designed to hinge upwards when not in use. The height of the canvas screen was also increased when compared to the Valentine. DD Shermans were used, with some patchy success, on D-Day, as well as during the Rhine crossing in 1945.

Shermans were also successfully adapted to carry the much-feared flame-thrower weapon.

Back in 1940 the British company Lagonda Motors had constructed and demonstrated a portable flame-thrower device that could project burning petroleum-based fuel a distance of 100ft, and eventually managed to extend this range to around 350ft. It was initially imagined that the weapon could be used for the protection of shipping and airfields against low-level attack by aircraft, but neither the Royal Navy nor the Royal Air Force showed much interest and further development concentrated on mounting the flame-thrower on either a truck or a tracked vehicle. In this form the British Petroleum Warfare Department (PWD) hoped that the weapon would prove to be effective against pillboxes and strong points. By the end of July 1942 the flame-thrower had been successfully adapted to allow it to be fitted to a tank, and versions were produced using both the Valentine and the Churchill, the latter carrying the flame-thrower fuel in a trailer. Known as the Churchill Crocodile, this version was selected for production, but the British and Canadian Armies also produced experimental Sherman flame-throwers under the names Ronson, Salamander and Adder.

The US Army similarly produced flame-thrower devices that could be mounted on the Sherman. In some cases the flame projector was fitted into the co-driver's periscope aperture or the hull machine-gun position, while in other cases it replaced the main gun. In late 1944 the US 2nd Armored Division also adapted four Shermans to mount the Churchill Crocodile flame-thrower.

Another role in which the Sherman was hugely successful was that of mine clearance. Large numbers of anti-tank mines were laid by the opposing armies, and in addition thousands of anti-personnel or land mines also presented considerable danger to the advancing armies. Various solutions to the problem of dealing with these mines were proposed, including explosive devices, flails, rollers and ploughs, all of them designed to be attached to modified tank hulls. Many were immediately dismissed as being impractical, but others were developed to the point where they were quite successful. Of these, the flail proved to be the most effective.

Work on a mine flail had started in 1939 when the British Mechanization Board had proposed that anti-tank mines could be exploded in situ by means of weights attached to the ends of spring-steel strips; the strips were attached to a revolving drum carried ahead of a tank. It was quickly found that the device was more effective if the spring-steel strips and weights were replaced by revolving chains, and initial trials of what was described as the Baron Mk I were carried out with a Matilda II tank. This was followed by the Baron Mk II, which was equipped with a hydraulic raising and lowering system for the rotor. During 1942 a simpler flail device, dubbed Scorpion, was developed in the Middle East, and by the end of July 1943 Scorpion had been issued for user trials, before being abandoned. However, during the previous month there had been considerable progress with mounting a modified version of the Scorpion on a Sherman tank, and this became the most successful of the flails. Designated Crab, the first prototype was ready for trials in September 1943 and the system proved to be very effective at destroying mines and cutting barbed wire.

Other approaches to the problem of mine clearance included explosive devices, ploughs and rollers. The Sherman Snake and Conger were both explosive devices and consisted of a long hosepipe or cylinder of explosive material that was intended to be pushed across a minefield and detonated remotely, thus exploding the mines ahead of the advancing tank. A similar device, dubbed Tapeworm, consisted of a flexible hosepipe that was designed to be towed across the minefield by a flail tank; once in position, it was filled with liquid explosive and detonated.

Tank-mounted ploughs designed to expose anti-tank mines were developed before the Second World War by agricultural engineers John Fowler & Company, but despite considerable work the device never lived up to its original promise. The British 79th Armoured Division developed a version of the plough, dubbed Bullshorn, testing it in conjunction with a Sherman. It was eventually abandoned in favour of the flail, but a few Bullshorns were useful on D-Day for filling in craters caused by exploding mines.

Anti-mine rollers had been developed in the years immediately following the end of the First World War, and were designed to detonate mines by simulating the weight of a tank rolling over the fuze. By 1937 John Fowler & Company had successfully trialled an anti-mine roller attachment (AMRA) consisting of a girder frame that was effectively pushed ahead of a tank, and which carried four heavy rollers. This idea was adapted to produce the Sherman-mounted anti-mine reconnaissance castor roller (AMRCR), which proved useful against anti-personnel mines. Spiked rollers were also tested experimentally in the Middle East, and one such device, dubbed Porcupine, was trialled in Britain in conjunction with a Sherman.

The most successful anti-mine roller was the Canadian indestructible roller device (CIRD). Constructed at the Canadian Army Workshops at Borden during 1943, the CIRD consisted of two rollers of solid forged armour-quality steel, 16in wide and with a diameter of 26in, each weighing around a ton. The rollers were carried on trailing arms suspended on a substantial cross-shaft, arranged to pivot some distance ahead of the tank in front of each track. Helical springs were provided to hold the trailing arms in the operating position. The CIRD was standardised for use with both the Sherman and the Churchill in May 1945, although further development of roller devices was eventually abandoned in favour of the more successful flail. Nevertheless, other roller devices such as Rodent, Aunt Jemima, Earthworm, Centipede and Lulu all achieved some degree of success. The last named brought a little more technology to the problem by adapting the successful Polish electro-magnetic mine-detection system for use with a tank. Finally the remote 'mine roller T10' replaced the track system of the Sherman with three huge rollers mounted tricycle fashion on swing arms.

The Sherman was also used, at least by the US Army, as a rocket-launcher mount. Various systems were developed, but only two – the 'T34 Calliope' and 'T40 Whizbang' – saw combat use. Dating from 1943 and used by the US 2nd Armored Division in France in 1944, Calliope consisted of sixty 4.6in rocket tubes mounted in a frame above the turret; the mount could rotate with the turret and the tubes were elevated by a mechanical link to the gun barrel. Whizbang was also used in combat in 1944/45, and consisted of twenty 7.2in rockets in a hydraulically elevated box mount.

Consideration was also given to adapting the Sherman to provide what the British would have described as an assault vehicle or 'armoured engineers' vehicle', and in April of 1945 a prototype was produced for the 'demolition tank T31'. The vehicle was constructed on an M4A3 chassis with the horizontal volute spring suspension (HVSS) system; the thickness of the floor was increased to 1.5in and both a flame projector and a 'dozer blade were fitted. The massive turret mounted a 105mm howitzer, with a 7.2in T94 rocket-launcher to either side; the rocket launcher incorporated a revolving feed mechanism that held five rounds, and reloading could be carried out from inside the hull. A single prototype, with a dummy 105mm gun, was delivered to Aberdeen Proving Ground in August 1945, but the project did not extend beyond the prototype stage and was subsequently cancelled.

Lastly, mention must be made of the inflatable canvas and rubber 'Shermans' that were deployed in 1943/44 as part of 'Operation Fortitude' – the deception plan that fooled the Germans into thinking that the invasion would come from Kent into the Pas de Calais region of France. All kinds of tactics were used, including dummy tanks and aircraft, fake radio traffic, and even the recorded sound of heavy trucks apparently moving around dummy marshalling areas. Comprising four separately inflated chambers, the dummy 'Shermans' were given realistic markings, as well as having nuts and bolts and other detail painted onto the canvas. Once inflated, the dummy 'tanks' were lined up in rows and covered with camouflage netting. Inflatable 'Shermans' were also used during 'Operation Shingle' at Anzio, in an attempt to confuse the enemy regarding the real location of Allied tanks.

The M32 tank recovery vehicle was the only Sherman engineer tank variant to be produced in volume. Changes from the standard gun tank specification included the addition of a large, fixed superstructure in place of the turret, and an 81mm smoke-laying mortar fitted to the top of the hull. There was a 60,000lb winch in the fighting compartment, and a pivoting A-frame jib on the hull. The photograph shows the M32B1 variant using the cast M4A1 chassis. (*Warehouse Collection*)

The British-designed Sherman ARV Mk II incorporated a Croft 60-ton winch in the fighting compartment, a detachable 3.5-ton winch at the front and a fixed 9.5-ton winch at the rear. There was also a substantial earth anchor and a fixed 'turret' in which was installed a dummy gun. (*Warehouse Collection*)

The Sherman beach armoured recovery vehicle (BARV) was designed to provide assistance to disabled vehicles on the Normandy landing beaches. The raised superstructure provides some protection against small arms fire and also allows the BARV to operate in up to 8ft of water. (*Warehouse Collection*)

Duplex-drive (DD) Shermans were designed for amphibious landing. The rubberised-canvas screen can be raised to allow the tank to float, while twin propeller drive provides a means of propulsion in the water. (*Firestone Tire & Rubber Company*)

(*Opposite top*) The flame-thrower is a very effective weapon against entrenched infantry. This Sherman M4A3E8, photographed in Korea, has been equipped with a flame projector – possibly the US Marine Corps POA-CWS 75 H1 device – operating through the barrel of the main gun. (*US Signal Corps*)

(*Opposite below*) The most effective Sherman-based anti-mine device was the chain flail, consisting of a large cylinder carried ahead of the tank to which were attached a series of chains. In this photograph the side covers of the flail have been removed to show the chain drive. (*Warehouse Collection*)

A flail can clear a path through a minefield sufficiently wide to permit following tanks or infantry to pass safely. (*Warehouse Collection*)

This improvised US Marine Corps mine flail was constructed using parts of the M1 'dozer kit. (*Warehouse Collection*)

The Canadian indestructible roller device (CIRD) consisted of two rollers of solid forged armour-quality steel, 16in wide and 26in in diameter. The rollers, which were sufficiently heavy to detonate mines, were carried on trailing arms suspended on a cross-shaft, pivoting ahead of the tank in front of each track; helical springs held the trailing arms in the operating position. (*Warehouse Collection*)

When the CIRD encounters a mine, the roller is thrown upwards by the blast, rotating around the cross-shaft. As the tank continues to move forward, spuds on the roller arm dig into the ground, and the roller is returned to its original position. (*Warehouse Collection*)

Mounted on the sides of the Sherman turret and attached to the gun barrel to allow elevation, the T34 Calliope rocket launcher carried sixty 4.6in rocket tubes in a frame. (*Tank Museum*)

'Demolition tank T31' was constructed on an M4A3E8 chassis. A flame projector and 'dozer blade were fitted, and the turret mounted a 105mm howitzer, with a 7.2in T94 rocket-launcher to either side. A single prototype, with a dummy gun, was delivered to Aberdeen Proving Ground in August 1945. (*Tank Museum*)

Inflatable 'tanks' were used in Britain and the Far East in order to confuse enemy aircraft regarding the numbers and locations of Allied armour. (*US Signal Corps*)

Chapter Eight

Sherman-Based Gun Motor Carriages

The general reliability of the M4 hull, chassis and running gear also made it the ideal candidate for adaptation to the role of gun motor carriage, or self-propelled gun. Examples include the M7B1 105mm gun motor carriage, the M36 90mm gun motor carriage, the M40 155mm gun motor carriage, the M43 8in howitzer motor carriage, the T51 25-pounder gun motor carriage, and the T94 10in howitzer motor carriage. The M10 tank destroyer also largely embraced the Sherman running gear, as did the M10A1 prime mover and the T30 cargo carrier. In addition, there was also a range of experimental vehicles that never entered production.

In June 1941 work started on developing what became the M7 105mm howitzer gun motor carriage using the lower hull and running gear of the M3 medium tank. Two prototypes, described as T32, were constructed at the Baldwin Locomotive Works, mounting the M1A2 105mm howitzer. Approval for production was given the following year, but when the M3 was superseded by the M4, production switched to the hull of the M4A3 and the designation was amended to M7B1. In line with their policy of assigning ecclesiastical names to self-propelled guns, the British dubbed this vehicle the Priest ... which meant that when the Canadian Army used a number of Priests that had been stripped of their guns and converted into Kangaroo armoured personnel carriers during 'Operation Totalise' in August 1944, they were inevitably dubbed 'defrocked Priests'! A total of 826 examples were built by Pressed Steel between March 1944 and February 1945, and 127 were built by Federal Machine & Welder.

Development of the M36 90mm gun motor carriage – sometimes referred to as the Jackson – started in late 1942. The first prototype, consisting of the hull of the M10A1 tank destroyer mounting a 90mm M3 high-velocity anti-tank gun in a new, larger turret, was completed in early 1943, and the design was standardised in June 1944. A total of 1,218 examples were constructed, with most converted from existing M10s, by the Fisher Tank Arsenal, the American Locomotive Company,

Massey-Harris and the Montreal Locomotive Works. Production ended in June 1945. The similar M36B1 also mounted the 90mm gun, but was constructed using the M4A3 hull, with 187 examples constructed by the Fisher Tank Arsenal in late 1944; and the M36B2 utilised the hull of the M10, with 237 examples constructed by the American Locomotive Company.

The M40 155mm gun motor carriage was based on a widened M4A3 chassis with the horizontal volute spring suspension (HVSS) system, and mounted the 155mm M1 howitzer. The pilot model, designated T83, was constructed in March 1944 and the Pressed Steel Car Company produced the first of five pilot vehicles in July 1944, before starting production of the first 300 in January 1945. The design was standardised in March that year. The contract was subsequently increased to cover 600 vehicles, but only 418 had been completed when the war ended. Twenty-four of the vehicles were subsequently converted to T89 8in gun motor carriage form. The contract for the remaining vehicles was terminated.

The requirement for the T89 8in gun motor carriage had arisen during tests of the first T83 pilot vehicle at Aberdeen Proving Ground, when the 155mm gun had been replaced by the 8in M1 howitzer to allow this weapon to be evaluated in a vehicle mount. The resulting vehicle was initially identified as the T89 8in gun motor carriage, and was designed in such a way that it could mount either the 155mm or the 8in gun. Although the design was standardised in August 1945, only 48 of the planned 576 examples were constructed, by the Pressed Steel Car Company, before production was halted in November 1945.

Although it could be argued that it was not really constructed on a Sherman chassis, the British Sexton self-propelled gun used the lower hull of the Canadian Ram II tank, with the turret and main gun removed to provide a mount for the British 25-pounder. Two 'marks' were produced, with detail variations, and a total of 2,150 were constructed by the Montreal Locomotive Works.

There were other Sherman-based projects that never really progressed beyond the prototype stage. The T30 cargo carrier, for example, was designed as a limber for the M40 155mm gun motor carriage, and just five examples were constructed by the Pressed Steel Car Company using the welded hull of the late model M4 with the horizontal volute spring suspension (HVSS) system before the project was terminated. Another still-born project was an American attempt at fitting the British 25-pounder gun into the M4 Sherman chassis. Dating from 1943 and designated T51, the development programme was abandoned following the destruction of the gun mount on the prototype during the first live-firing exercise. Similarly abortive, but this time because the performance was not felt to be acceptable, was the T52 multiple gun motor carriage. This carried either two 40mm anti-aircraft guns or a single 40mm cannon flanked by a pair of 0.50in machine guns, and was designed for the anti-aircraft role. Work on the project had started in July 1942 but was terminated in October 1944. Finally, the T53 90mm gun motor carriage, also intended for anti-aircraft use, also failed to reach fruition. Work on this project had started in July 1942, using an M4 chassis that had been modified to place the engine at the centre, with a 90mm gun at the rear. This proved unsatisfactory, and the subsequent T53E1 variant, which was intended for both anti-aircraft and anti-tank roles, saw the engine moved back to its normal position, and the gun placed at the centre. The project was abandoned in May 1944.

The M10 tank destroyer should also be considered a close relative of the Sherman. Development started in April 1942 under the project designation T35, with the first prototype based on an M4A2 hull to which had been fitted an open-topped turret. When this was rejected, a second vehicle – the T35E1 – was constructed using the lower part of the M4A2 hull, with a relatively lightweight angled upper superstructure carrying a five-sided open-topped turret mounting the highly accurate 3in M7 anti-tank gun. The turret was always considered to be unbalanced and required a large counterweight at the rear, but the design was standardised in June 1942 and production started in September using both M4A2 and M4A3 chassis, the latter being designated M10A1. A total of 6,706 vehicles were constructed before production was terminated in November 1943: 5,668 examples, including both the M10 and the M10A1, were constructed at the Fisher Tank Arsenal, and 738 M10A1s by the Ford Motor Company. In an attempt to overcome the lack of balance in the turret, a further pilot vehicle was produced, designated T72, using a version of the turret from the T23 medium tank, mounting a 3in main gun. This project was eventually abandoned in favour of the Buick M18 Hellcat.

Examples of the M10 and the M10A1 were supplied to the British Army where they were dubbed Wolverine, but from late 1944 many of those remaining in service had the 3in M7 gun replaced by the more powerful British OQF 17-pounder (76.2mm) at the Royal Ordnance Factory, Woolwich (the same weapon that was installed in the Firefly). The resulting vehicle, which packed a considerably bigger punch than the original M10, was dubbed Achilles, and many of these remained in service well into the post-war years. Others had the gun and turret removed and were converted to artillery tractors.

The M7 gun motor carriage – or Priest – used the Sherman lower hull and running gear to mount a 105mm howitzer. Production started in 1942. (*US Signal Corps*)

(*Opposite top*) With the later one-piece cast nose, this Priest was designated M7B1. The vehicle is preserved at Aberdeen Proving Ground. (*Yellowute*)

(*Opposite below*) Often dubbed 'Big Shot', the fearsome M40 gun motor carriage was equipped with the American 155mm howitzer, and was designed for bombardment support of advancing armoured divisions. (*Mark Pelligrini*)

The British Sexton 25-pounder self-propelled gun used the hull and running gear of the Canadian Ram II tank, although, being derived from the American M3 Lee/Grant medium tank, it was broadly similar to that of the Sherman. (*Simon Thomson*)

Photographed alongside the M4 Sherman for comparison, the M10 gun motor carriage – sometimes called Wolverine by the British – carried a 3in anti-tank gun in an open-topped turret. The angled superstructure of the upper hull ensured a low silhouette. (*General Motors Corporation*)

An M36 gun motor carriage in Korea. Most M36s were converted from redundant M10A1 hulls, which in turn were derived from the M4A3; the M36B2 was based on the M10 hull, which was based on the M4A2. (*US Signal Corps*)

Powered by the GM 6046D twin diesel engine or the Ford GAA-III, the M36 gun motor carriage was effectively an M10 onto which had been mounted a new turret carrying a 90mm anti-aircraft gun. (*Simon Thomson*)

The British Achilles self-propelled gun was an American M10 to which had been fitted the more powerful British OQF 17-pounder (76.2mm) gun. In this photograph the turret is traversed to the rear. (*Warehouse Collection*)

Rear view of the Achilles self-propelled gun. With the 3in gun replaced by the 17-pounder (76.2mm), the vehicle became a potent tank destroyer. Many remained in post-war service with the British Army. (*Warehouse Collection*)

Appendix

Sherman Reference Data

TECHNICAL SPECIFICATION

Typical nomenclature: tank, medium, M4, M4A1, M4A2, M4A3, M4A4, M4A6; generally described as Sherman, or General Sherman; and, tank, medium, M4A5, Grizzly.
Prototypes manufactured by: Aberdeen Proving Ground, Rock Island Arsenal.
Production vehicles manufactured by: American Locomotive Company (ALCO), Baldwin Locomotive Works, Chrysler Detroit Tank Arsenal (DTAP), Federal Machine & Welder Company, Ford Motor Company, GM Fisher Tank Arsenal, Lima Locomotive Works, Montreal Locomotive Works, Pacific Car & Foundry Company, Pressed Steel Car Company and Pullman-Standard Car Manufacturing Company.
Engines produced by: Caterpillar Tractor Company, Chrysler Corporation, Continental Aircraft Engine Company, General Motors Detroit Diesel Division, Ford Motor Company and the Wright Aeronautical Division of the Curtiss-Wright Corporation.
Total number produced: 49,422, all variants.
Production: 1942–45.

MAIN ENGINE

M4, M4A1, M4A5 Grizzly: Wright or Continental R-975-EC2, R-975-C1 or R-975-C4; nine-cylinder supercharged radial petrol engine; bore and stroke, 5.0in × 5.5in; capacity, 15,928cc (972in³); compression ratio, 5.7:1 or 6.3:1; overhead valves; gross power output, (R-975-EC2 and R-975-C1) 340bhp at 2,400rpm, (R-975-C4) 400bhp at 2,400rpm; maximum torque, (R-975-EC2 and R-975-C1) 890lbf/ft at 1,800rpm, (R-975-C4) 1,025lbf/ft at 1,800rpm.
M4A2: GM 6046D; twin 6-71 in-line six-cylinder two-stroke supercharged diesel engines, installed side-by-side; bore and stroke, 4.25in × 5.0in; capacity, 13,929cc (850in³); compression ratio, 16:1; overhead valves; gross power output, 410bhp at 2,900rpm; maximum torque, 1,000lbf/ft at 1,400rpm.
M4A3: Ford GAA-III; normally aspirated 60-degree V8 petrol engine; bore and stroke, 5.4in × 6.0in; capacity, 18,026cc (1,100in³); compression ratio, 7.5:1; overhead valves, four per cylinder; gross power output, 500bhp at 2,600rpm; maximum torque, 1,040lbf/ft at 2,200rpm.

M4A4: Chrysler A-57 multi-bank; thirty cylinders arranged in five in-line banks of six around a common crankcase; bore and stroke, 4.37in x 4.5in; (combined) capacity, 20,533cc (1,253in³); compression ratio, 6:21; side valves; gross power output, 425bhp at 2,850rpm; maximum torque, 1,020lbf/ft at 1,200rpm.

M4A6: Caterpillar D-200A (RD-1820); nine-cylinder radial supercharged multi-fuel diesel engine; bore and stroke, 6.125in x 6.875in; capacity, 29,874cc (1,823in³); compression ratio, 15.5:1; overhead valves; gross power output, 450bhp at 2,000rpm; maximum torque, 1,470lbf/ft at 1,200rpm.

AUXILIARY ENGINE

Homelite HRUH-28 single-cylinder two-stroke air-cooled petrol engine, coupled to a 30V 50A generator designed to charge the batteries; bore and stroke, 2.375in x 2.125in; capacity, 154cc (9.4in³).

TRANSMISSION AND STEERING SYSTEM

Gearbox: constant-mesh five-speed (5F1R), with manual shift. Manufactured by Buick, Caterpillar Tractor, Detroit Tank Arsenal, Ford Motor Company, Iowa Transmission and Reed Roller Bit Company. Gearbox arranged to drive the front sprockets through a twin-plate dry-plate clutch manufactured by Borg & Beck, or Lipe.

Gearbox ratios: first gear, 7.56:1; second gear, 3.11:1; third gear, 1.78:1; fourth gear, 1.11:1; fifth gear, 0.73:1; reverse gear, 5.65:1.

Steering system: bevel-gear controlled differential.

Final drive: herringbone reduction gear train; final ratio 2.84:1; drive sprocket at front.

Minimum turning radius: 32ft.

SUSPENSION

Early tanks used the 'vertical volute spring suspension' (VVSS) system, arranged as three bogies on either side, each comprising a pair of leading and trailing radial arms acting on twin vertical volute springs. From March 1944 the suspension was modified to incorporate horizontal springs; this was known as the 'horizontal volute spring suspension' (HVSS) system; the twin springs were placed side by side, with a large hydraulic telescopic shock absorber above.

Road wheels: 20in diameter, rubber-tyred; six wheels (VVSS), or six pairs of wheels (HVSS) on each side.

Tracks: cast manganese steel, running on three track-return rollers and rear idler; several patterns of both steel and rubber-faced tracks were used during the design life of the vehicle.

BRAKES AND STEERING
Mechanically operated, acting on the outside of brake drums carried on the differential output shafts.

CONSTRUCTION
Cast, welded, or composite cast/welded steel hull; *appliqué* armour added to various areas, both during manufacture and in the field; one-piece cast turret with welded roof.

CAPACITIES
Fuel capacity: 124–146gal (148–175 US gal), according to variant.
Oil capacity: M4, M4A1, M4A5, 7.5gal (9 US gal); M4A2, 5.8gal (7 US gal); M4A3, M4A4, 6.67gal (8 US gal); M4A4, 12.9gal (15.5 US gal).
Cooling system capacity: 11.66gal (14 US gal); M4, M4A1 and M4A5 are air-cooled
Electrical system: 24V, wired on a negative earth system, using two 6V batteries; 12V system provided for radio equipment.

PERFORMANCE
Maximum speed: on roads, 24–30mph.
Fuel consumption: 0.6 mpg average.
Maximum range: on roads, 100–150 miles.
Maximum gradient: 60 degrees at full tractive effort.
Side slope: 30 per cent.
Vertical obstacle: 24in.
Trench crossing: 89in.
Fording depth: unprepared, 36–40in; prepared, 48in.
Maximum gun elevation: 75mm gun, +25 degrees; 76mm gun, +25 degrees; 105mm gun, +35 degrees; 17-pounder (76.2mm) gun, +20 degrees.
Maximum gun depression: 75mm gun, −12 degrees (−10 degrees with mount M34A1); 76mm gun, −12 degrees; 105mm gun, −10 degrees; 17-pounder (76.2mm) gun, −5 degrees.

DIMENSIONS AND WEIGHT
Dimensions: length, 230–248in (hull only, with sand shields), 232–298in (gun forward, without sand shields), 232–287in (gun to the rear); width, 103–105in (with sand shields); height, over turret hatch or cupola, 108–117in.
Ground clearance: 17in.
Track width: 16.56in on VVSS suspension; 23 or 24in on HVSS suspension.
Track pitch: 6in pitch; M4A5 only, 4.6in.

Track centres: 83–89in.

Bogie centres: 57in (63.625in for M4A4 and M4A6).

Number of track shoes: 79 (83 for M4A4 and M4A6).

Length of track on ground: 147in (160in for M4A4 and M4A6).

Combat weight: 66,900–72,900lb (M4A3E2, 84,000lb).

Ground pressure: 13.4–14.2lbf/in².

Power to weight ratio: 12.0–14.2bhp/ton.

Bridge classification: 40.

Thickness of hull armour: front upper surface, 51 or 64mm (M4A3E2, 102mm); front lower surface, 51–108mm (M4A3E2, 140mm); sides, 38mm (M4A3E2, 38–76mm); rear areas, 38mm; floor, 13–25mm.

Thickness of turret: front, 64–76mm (M4A3E2, 152mm); sides and rear, 51–76mm (M4A3E2, 152mm); roof, 25mm.

Table 1. Major Sherman gun tank variants

Variant: US designation	British designation	Date	Engine (petrol engine unless otherwise indicated)	Suspension	Hull	Max armour thickness: hull	turret	Main gun	Weight: unstowed	combat
M4	Sherman I	1942	Wright or Continental R-975 radial; 400bhp	VVSS	welded	51mm	76mm	75mm M3	66,900lb	62,800lb
M4 'composite'	Sherman I hybrid	1942	Wright or Continental R-975 radial; 400bhp	VVSS	rolled/cast	51mm	89mm	75mm M3	66,900lb	62,800lb
M4 (105mm)	Sherman IB	1943	Wright or Continental R-975 radial; 400bhp	VVSS	welded	64mm	91mm	105mm M4	69,400lb	62,300lb
M4 (105mm)	Sherman IBY	1944	Wright or Continental R-975 radial; 400bhp	HVSS	welded	51mm	76mm	105mm M4	69,400lb	62,800lb
M4E1 (ii)	-	1942	Caterpillar D-200 (RD-1820) radial diesel; 450bhp	VVSS	welded	51mm	76mm	75mm M3	n/a	n/a
M4A1	Sherman II	1942	Wright or Continental R-975 radial; 400bhp	VVSS	cast	51mm	76mm	75mm M2; 75mm M3	66,800lb	62,700lb
M4A1E4 (76mm)	Sherman IIA	1944	Wright or Continental R-975 radial; 400bhp	VVSS	cast	108mm	91mm	76mm M1	70,600lb	64,600lb
M4A1E8 (76mm)	Sherman IIAY	1944	Wright or Continental R-975 radial; 400bhp	HVSS	cast	108mm	91mm	76mm M1	70,600lb	64,600lb
M4A2	Sherman III	1942	GM 6046D diesel; 410bhp (2x 6-71, 205bhp)	VVSS	welded	108mm	89mm	75mm M3	69,000lb	66,000lb
M4A2 (76mm)	Sherman IIIA	1944	GM 6046D diesel; 410bhp (2x 6-71, 205bhp)	VVSS	welded	108mm	89mm	76mm M1	73,400lb	67,300lb
M4A2E8 (76mm)	Sherman IIIAY	1944	GM 6046D diesel; 410bhp (2x 6-71, 205bhp)	HVSS	welded	108mm	89mm	76mm M1	73,400lb	67,300lb
M4A3	Sherman IV	1942	Ford GAA-III V8; 450bhp	VVSS	welded	51mm	89mm	75mm M3	66,700lb	62,500lb
M4A3 (105mm)	Sherman IVB	1942	Ford GAA-III V8; 450bhp	VVSS	welded	108mm	91mm	105mm M4	72,900lb	66,400lb
M4A3E2 'Jumbo'	-	1944	Ford GAA-III V8; 450bhp	VVSS	welded	140mm	178mm	75mm M3; 76mm M1*	84,000lb	77,500lb
M4A3E4 (76mm)	Sherman IVAY	1944	Ford GAA-III V8; 450bhp	HVSS	welded	108mm	89mm	76mm M1	69,600lb	64,000lb
M4A3E8 (76mm)	Sherman IVAY	1944	Ford GAA-III V8; 450bhp	HVSS	welded	108mm	89mm	76mm M1	74,200lb	68,100lb
M4A3E9 (105mm)	Sherman IVBY	1942	Ford GAA-III V8; 450bhp	HVSS	welded	108mm	91mm	105mm M4	72,900lb	66,400lb
M4A4	Sherman V	1942	Chrysler A-57 multi-bank; 425bhp (5x 85bhp)	VVSS	welded	51mm	76mm	75mm M3	69,700lb	65,400lb
M4A5 Grizzly	Sherman VI**	1943	Wright or Continental R-975 radial; 400bhp	VVSS	cast	75mm	76mm	75mm M3	66,500lb	62,400lb
M4A6	Sherman VII	1943	Caterpillar D-200 (RD-1820) radial diesel; 450bhp	VVSS	rolled/cast	108mm	89mm	75mm M3	70,000lb	65,800lb

* 76mm gun sometimes fitted as field modification.
** This designation allocated but not used.

Table 2. Development vehicles

Designation	Date	Description
M4E1 (i)	1942	M4A1 fitted with 76mm T1 gun in the standard turret; T23 turret subsequently used
M4E1 (ii)	1942	M4A4 fitted with Caterpillar D200-A (RD-1820) radial diesel engine; subsequently adopted as M4A6
M4E2	1943	M4A4 fitted with 24in wide T80 track and HVSS suspension
M4E3	1943	M4A4 fitted with Chrysler V12 engine
M4E4	1943	M4 fitted with 24in wide tracks and torsion-bar suspension
M4E5	1943	M4 prototyped with 105mm howitzer
M4E6	1943	Pilot vehicle fitted with T23 turret with M1 76mm gun and wet ammunition stowage
M4E7	1943	M4A1 fitted with Ford GAA-III engine
M4E8	1943	M4A3 fitted with HVSS and 76mm gun
M4E9	1943	M4 fitted with spaced VVSS suspension and bolt-on grousers
M4A1E1	n/a	M4A1 with aluminium foil heat-reflective insulation and air-conditioning system for desert combat
M4A1E2	n/a	M4A1 fitted with recording odograph and infrared lights for night fighting
M4A1E3	n/a	M4A1 fitted with Spicer Model 95 torque converter in place of standard clutch
M4A1E4	n/a	M4A1 fitted with 76mm gun
M4A1E5	n/a	M4A1 with improved Continental R-975-C4 radial engine and increased fuel capacity; subsequently adopted for late production
M4A1E8	1944	Prototype for late production M4A1 with HVSS and wet ammunition stowage
M4A1E9	1944	M4A1 fitted with spaced VVSS suspension and bolt-on grousers
M4A2E1	1943	M4A2 fitted with GM V8 diesel engine
M4A2E4	1943	M4A2 fitted with 24in wide tracks and torsion-bar suspension
M4A2E9	1943	M4A2 fitted with spaced VVSS suspension and bolt-on grousers
M4A3E1	1944	M4A3 fitted with Spicer Model 95 torque converter in place of standard clutch
M4A3E2	1944	Prototype for heavy assault tank – known as 'Jumbo' or 'Cobra King'
M4A3E3	1944	Prototype M4A3 with 47 degrees frontal armour
M4A3E8	1944	Prototype M4A3 with 76mm gun, HVSS and wet ammunition stowage
M4A3E9	1944	M4A3 fitted with spaced VVSS suspension and bolt-on grousers
M4A4E1	1942	M4A4 prototyped with 105mm howitzer

Table 3. Engine specifications

	Caterpillar D-200A (RD-1820) radial	Chrysler A-57 multi-bank	Continental or Wright R-975-EC2 or C1	Continental or Wright R-975-C4	Ford GAA-III V8	GM 6046D twin 6-71 diesels
Application	M4A6	M4A4	M4, M4A1	M4, M4A1, M4A5 Grizzly	M4A3	M4A2
Capacity	29,874cc (1,823in³)	20,533cc (1,253in³)	15,928cc (972in³)	15,928cc (972in³)	18,026cc (1,100in³)	13,929cc (850in³)
Number of cylinders	R9	30 (5x in-line six)	R9	R9	V8, 60 deg	12 (2x in-line six)
Bore and stroke	6.125 x 6.875in	4.37 x 4.5in	5 x 5.5in	5 x 5.5in	5.4 x 6in	4.25 x 5in
Compression ratio	15.5:1	6.2:1	6.3:1, 5.7:1*	5.7:1	7.5:1	16:1
Rotation (from nose end)	anti-clockwise	anti-clockwise	anti-clockwise	anti-clockwise	anti-clockwise	anti-clockwise
Maximum governed speed	2,000rpm	2,850rpm	2,400rpm	2,400rpm	2,600rpm	2,100rpm
Gross power output	497bhp at 2,000rpm	425bhp at 2,850rpm	400bhp at 2,400rpm	460bhp at 2,400rpm	500bhp at 2,600rpm	410bhp at 2,900rpm
Net power output	450bhp at 2,000rpm	370bhp at 2,400rpm	340bhp at 2,400rpm	400bhp at 2,400rpm	450bhp at 2,600rpm	375bhp at 2,100rpm
Maximum gross torque	1,470lbf/ft at 1,200rpm	1,060lbf/ft at 1,400rpm	890lbf/ft at 1,800rpm	1,025lbf/ft at 1,800rpm	1,040lbf/ft at 2,200rpm	1,000lbf/ft at 1,400rpm
Net torque	945lbf/ft at 2,100rpm	1,020lbf/ft at 1,200rpm	800lbf/ft at 1,800rpm	940lbf/ft at 1,700rpm	950lbf/ft at 2,200rpm	885lbf/ft at 1,900rpm
Number of cycles	four	four	four	four	four	two
Fuel	diesel, 40 cetane	petrol, 80 octane	petrol, 92 or 80 octane*	petrol, 80 octane	petrol, 80 octane	diesel, 40 cetane
Induction system	supercharged	normally aspirated	supercharged	supercharged	normally aspirated	supercharged
Ignition system	compression	battery	magneto	magneto	magneto	compression
Lubrication system	dry sump	dry sump	dry sump	dry sump	wet sump	wet sump
Cooling system	air	water	air	air	water	water
Length	56in	54.125in	53in	53in	60.375in	65.625in
Width	55in	58.75in	45in	45in	33.25in	59.375in
Height	55in	56.5in	45in	45in	47.5in	46.75in
Dry weight	3,536lb	5,400lb	1,137lb	1,137lb	1,560lb	5,110lb

* The R-975-EC2 engine had a compression ratio of 6.3:1 and required minimum 92-octane fuel.

Table 4. Armour thickness

Variant:	M4 75mm	M4 105mm	M4A1 75mm	M4A1 76mm	M4A2 75mm	M4A2 76mm	M4A3 75mm	M4A3 76mm	M4A3 105mm	M4A3E2 75mm	M4A4 75mm	M4A5 75mm	M4A6 75mm
Hull:													
Front upper	51mm	64mm	51mm	64mm	64mm	64mm	51mm*	64mm	64mm	102mm	51mm	51mm	51mm
(angle from vertical)	56 deg	47 deg	37–55 deg	37–55 deg	47 deg	47 deg	56 deg	47 deg	47 deg	47 deg	56 deg	37–55 deg	51 deg
Front lower	51mm	51–108mm	51mm	51–108mm	51–108mm	51–108mm	51mm*	51–108mm	51–108mm	114–140mm	51mm	51mm	51–108mm
(angle from vertical)	0–56 deg	0–56 deg	0–45°deg	0–56 deg	0–56 deg	0–56 deg	0–56 deg	0–56 deg	0–56 deg	0–56 deg	0–45 deg	0–45 deg	0–56 deg
Sides	38mm	38mm	38mm	38mm	38mm	38mm	38mm	38mm	38mm	38–76mm	38mm	38mm	38mm
Top	19mm	19mm	13–19mm	19mm	19mm	19mm	19mm	19mm	19mm	19mm	19mm	13–19mm	19mm
Rear	38mm	38mm	38mm	38mm	38mm	38mm	38mm	38mm	38mm	38mm	38mm	38mm	38mm
Floor, front	25mm	25mm	25mm	25mm	25mm	25mm	25mm	25mm	25mm	25mm	25mm	25mm	25mm
Floor, rear	13mm	13mm	13mm	13mm	13mm	13mm	13mm	13mm	13mm	13mm	13mm	13mm	13mm

Note: the effective thickness of the armour is increased by virtue of being sloped on various parts of the hull

Variant:	M4 75mm	M4 105mm	M4A1 75mm	M4A1 76mm	M4A2 75mm	M4A2 76mm	M4A3 75mm	M4A3 76mm	M4A3 105mm	M4A3E2 75mm	M4A4 75mm	M4A5 75mm	M4A6 75mm
Turret:													
Gun shield	89mm	91mm	76mm	89mm	89mm	89mm	89mm	89mm	89mm	178mm	76mm	76mm	89mm
Gun rotor shield	51mm	–	51mm	–	51mm	–	51mm	–	–	–	51mm	51mm	51mm
Front	76mm	76mm	76mm	64mm	76mm	64mm	76mm	64mm	76mm	152mm	76mm	76mm	76mm
Sides	51mm	51mm	76mm	64mm	51mm	64mm	51mm	64mm	51mm	152mm	51mm	76mm	51mm
Roof	25mm	25mm	25mm	25mm	25mm	25mm	25mm	25mm	25mm	25mm	25mm	25mm	25mm
Rear	51mm	51mm	51mm	64mm	51mm	64mm	51mm	64mm	51mm	152mm	51mm	51mm	51mm

* Figures increased to 64mm (front upper) and 51–108mm (front lower) for tanks with wet ammunition storage.

Table 5. Ammunition stowage: numbers of rounds carried

	Variant: M4 75mm	M4 105mm	M4A1 75mm	M4A1 76mm	M4A2 75mm	M4A2 76mm	M4A3 75mm*	M4A3 76mm	M4A3 105mm	M4A3E2 75mm	M4A4 75mm	M4A5 75mm	M4A6 75mm	Firefly VC 17-pounder
Mounted weapons:														
Main gun	97	66	90	71	97	71	97	71	66	104	97	90	97	77
0.30in machine gun	4,750	4,000	4,750	6,250	4,750	6,250	4,750	6,250	4,000	6,250	4,750	4,750	4,750	5,000
0.50in machine gun	300	600	300	600	300	600	300	600	600	600	300	300	300	1,170
2in smoke bombs	12	12	–	12	12	14	12	18	15	18	–	–	12	27
Crew's personal weapons:														
0.45in pistol	600	900	600	900	600	900	600	900	900	900	600	600	600	440
Hand grenades	12	12	12	12	12	12	12	12	12	12	12	12	12	9

* M4A3(75)W, with wet ammunition stowage: 104 rounds for main gun, 6,250x 0.30in machine-gun rounds, 600x 0.50in machine-gun rounds, 18x 2in smoke bombs.

Table 6. Numbers of Shermans constructed

Company	Variants and numbers constructed: M4 75mm	M4 105mm	M4A1 75mm	M4A1 76mm	M4A2 75mm	M4A2 76mm	M4A3 75mm	M4A3 76mm	M4A3 105mm	M4A3E2 75mm	M4A4 75mm	M4A5 75mm	M4A6 75mm
American Locomotive	2,150	–	–	–	150	–	–	–	–	–	–	–	–
Baldwin Locomotive	1,233	–	–	–	12	–	–	–	–	–	–	–	–
Chrysler (Detroit Tank Arsenal)	1,676	1,641	–	–	–	–	–	4,017	3,039	–	7,499	–	75
Federal Machine & Welder	–	–	–	–	540	–	–	–	–	–	–	–	–
GM (Fisher Tank Arsenal)	–	–	–	–	4,614	2,894	3,071	525	–	254	–	–	–
Ford Motor Company	–	–	–	–	–	–	1,690	–	–	–	–	–	–
Lima Locomotive	–	–	1,655	–	–	–	–	–	–	–	–	–	–
Montreal Locomotive Works	–	–	–	–	–	–	–	–	–	–	–	188	–
Pacific Car & Foundry	–	–	926	–	–	–	–	–	–	–	–	–	–
Pressed Steel Car	1,000	–	3,700	3,426	–	21	–	–	–	–	–	–	–
Pullman-Standard	689	–	–	–	2,737	–	–	–	–	–	–	–	–
Sub-totals	6,748	1,641	6,281	3,426	8,053	2,915	4,761	4,542	3,039	254	7,499	188	75
Total by variant	8,389		9,707		10,968		12,596			254	7,499	188	75

Grand total of Sherman production: USA, 49,234; Canada, 188

Table 7. Manufacturing contracts and serial numbers, 1941–45

Manufacturer	Contract number	Year(s)	USA numbers and serial numbers*
M4 variants			
American Locomotive	W-ORD-485	1941	USA 3033885–3034254; USA 3066484–3066983; USA 3033235–3034234; USA 3072902–3073201 Serial numbers: 4124–4473; 4305–4804; 24705–25704; 40305–40604
Baldwin Locomotive	W-ORD-1814	1941	USA 3022537–3023381 Serial numbers: 1917–2304; 15435–16279
Chrysler (Detroit Tank Arsenal)	W-ORD-461	1943–44	USA 3032037–3032434; USA 3098789–3099486; USA 30100462–30101041; USA 30103603–30104302; USA 30111769–30112183; USA 30120071–30120196; USA 30139426–30139825 Serial numbers: 60174–60571; 4255–43252; 44228–44807; 56921–57620; 58208–58622; 64132–64257; 73436–73835
Lima Locomotive	W-ORD-694	1942	USA 3058972–3059071; USA 3067630–3067901 Serial numbers: 25705–25804; 25805–26076
Pressed Steel Car	W-ORD-717	1942	USA 3015661–3015983; USA 3036535–3036760 Serial numbers: 32104–32204; 10660–10982; 28005–28230
Pullman-Standard	W-ORD-718	1942–43	USA 3080017–3088242; USA 3039872–3040334 Serial numbers: 6205–6430; 30205–30667
M4A1 variants			
Lima Locomotive	W-ORD-1159	1942	USA 3058317–3058971; USA 3038135–3038734 Serial numbers: 6805–7459; 29605–30204
Pacific Car & Foundry	W-ORD-2557	1942	USA 3060572–3061372; USA 3061373–3061497 Serial numbers: 3005–3804; 13460–13584
Pressed Steel Car	W-ORD-717	1941–45	USA 3014761–3015660; USA 3015984–3016460; USA 3036761–3038134; USA 3069497–3070496; USA 30133706–30135085 USA 3084447–3085277; USA 3070497–3071626; USA 30125680–30127006; USA 30135486–30135598; USA 30140226–30140435 Serial numbers: 5–904; 10983–11459; 28231–29604; 36900–37899; 31805–32103; 69874–71253; 51850–52680; 37900–39029; 67701–69027; 71654–71766; 73856–74045
M4A2 variants			
American Locomotive	W-ORD-485	1941	USA 3033735–3033884 Serial numbers: 4474–4623
Baldwin Locomotive	W-ORD-1814	1942	USA numbers not available Serial numbers: 1905–1916
Federal Machine & Welder	W-ORD-1261	1942	USA 3055965–3056504 Serial numbers: 14785–15324
GM (Fisher Tank Arsenal)	W-ORD-1241	1941–45	USA 3014311–3014359; USA 3020861–3021161; USA 3062709–3064708; USA 3064709–3064983; USA 3034835–3036486; USA 3036499–3036534; USA 3080152–3080440; USA 3080441–3081211; USA 30116407–30116801; USA 30116802–30117019; USA 30122237–30123236; USA 30129507–30130352; USA 30135599–30136448 Serial numbers: 2305–2353; 2354–2654; 7460–9459; 16280–16554; 26305–27956; 27969–28004; 47555–47843; 47844–43614; 63385–64779; 63780–63997; 64258–65257; 69028–69873; 71767–72616
Pressed Steel Car	W-ORD-717	1944–45	USA 30142759–30142908 Serial numbers: 76074–76223
Pullman-Standard	W-ORD-718	1941–42	USA 3053115–3053614; USA 3095651–3096850; USA 3038735–3039371; USA 3096851–3097250 Serial numbers: 905–1404; 9460–10659; 30668–31304; 13585–13984

Table 7. Manufacturing contracts and serial numbers, 1941–45 continued

M4A3 variants

Chrysler (Detroit Tank Arsenal)	W-ORD-461	1943–45	USA 30111184–30111768; USA 30103303–30103602; USA 30120197–30120328; USA 30124580–30125035; USA 30136724–30137267; USA 30140436–30142463 Serial numbers: 57623–58207; 56621–56920; 64000–64131; 65258–65713; 72892–73435; 74046–76073
GM Fisher Tank Arsenal	W-ORD-1241	1943–45	USA 30115882–30116406; USA 30123237–30123436; USA 30136599–30136723; USA 3082923–3083176 Serial numbers: 62860–63384; 67501–67700; 72767–72891; 50326–50579
Ford Motor Company	W-ORD-1213	1941–42	USA 3055615–3055964; USA 3053615–3054954 Serial numbers: 2655–3004; 11460–12799

M4A4 variants

Chrysler (Detroit Tank Arsenal)	W-ORD-461	1941	USA 3056615–3058014; USA 3016861–3020860; USA 3029082–3031158; USA 3031162–3031182 Serial numbers: 4805–6204; 16555–20554; 20555–22631; 22632–22652

M4A6 variants

Chrysler (Detroit Tank Arsenal)	W-ORD-461	1943	USA 3099687–3099761 Serial numbers: 43453–43527

* The table includes all available data, but is not necessarily comprehensive.

Table 8. Numbers of Shermans refurbished

Company	Variants and numbers refurbished: (no breakdown available to indicate gun types for refurbished tanks)			
	M4	M4A1	M4A2	M4A3
Chrysler, Detroit Tank Arsenal	1,610	–	–	–
Chrysler, Evansville plant	446	1,216	–	–
Federal Machine & Welder	–	–	317	–
GM Fisher Tank Arsenal	–	–	218	–
IH Quad Cities Tank Arsenal	289	737	–	–
Montreal Locomotive Works	–	–	–	400
US Army Tank Depots	60	306	–	28
Grand total of Sherman refurbishment: 5,880				